WHAT? ME TEACH MUSIC?

A CLASSROOM TEACHER'S GUIDE TO MUSIC IN EARLY CHILDHOOD

Marjorie Lawrence

Alfred

MARJORIE LAWRENCE
Biography

Marjorie Lawrence, a native Texan, is a veteran teacher whose experience spans over forty years, ranging from a teen-aged country school teacher to her present position as State Elementary Chairman and a Vice-President of the Texas Music Educators Association.

Her background as a classroom teacher, music specialist, play school director and church school music director was a determining factor in the content and format of the early education music guide. Her basic philosophy, "to keep your sense of humor and your common sense" can be felt throughout the pages.

Mrs. Lawrence holds a Bachelor's degree from the University of Houston, and a Master's degree from the University of Houston at Clear Lake City. She received her music certificate from Sam Houston State University in Huntsville, Texas, and her early education certificate from the University of Houston at Clear Lake City. She has Orff and Kodaly certificates and has done additional graduate work in this area at Colorado State University.

Table of Contents

A SPECIAL "THANK YOU!"

To my peers who gave hours of their time editing and making helpful suggestions: ("Why in the world did you put *that* in here?")

To my husband who never knew quite what was going on.

To my mother who knew it was perfect before I ever started.

But mostly—
To Nancy and *Jay Green* who don't know a note of music but without whose merciless goading I never would have

M—a—d—e————it.

M.L.

A Special Thank You
for
A Special Person,
Grace Nash

who has combined, gleaned, inspired, researched, written, motivated, composed, created, and served up a completely Americanized in-depth music program.

She has extensive publications in areas of movement, speech, singing, body percussion, and use of mallet instruments.

WHAT? Me Teach MUSIC??!

You gotta be kidding!

HELP!!

Pull yourself together—

   You will find it's the happiest part of the day!

   Here's the help that you need.

Painless?   We promise!   Progressive (Mostly)

   Prepared?   Instant! Just add love and enthusiasm!

Preface

Many schools do not have music specialists for pre-school and primary children, and the classroom teacher is required to teach her own music.

In spite of the volumes of published music, resource materials and in-depth guides available, a teacher who does not know music may become overwhelmed with what she encounters.

Also, with her limited time she cannot analyze and make appropriate choices in song material. Often a selection is made because a song is "cute," even though the rhythm and melody may be impossible for a small child to handle.

Purpose

The purpose of this book is to present a first-level "pick-up-and-use" guide that a person with no music background can use with success.

All materials have been carefully chosen to provide a core foundation that a music specialist can build on later.

The very important step of *preparation* can be done by you!

Introduction

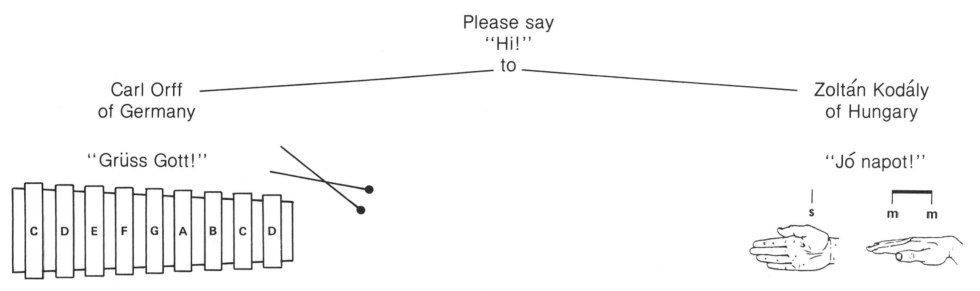

Please say
"Hi!"
to

Carl Orff ———————————————————— Zoltán Kodály
of Germany   of Hungary

"Grüss Gott!"   "Jó napot!"

This material is based on their philosophies and pedagogy of teaching.

The Basic Music Approach

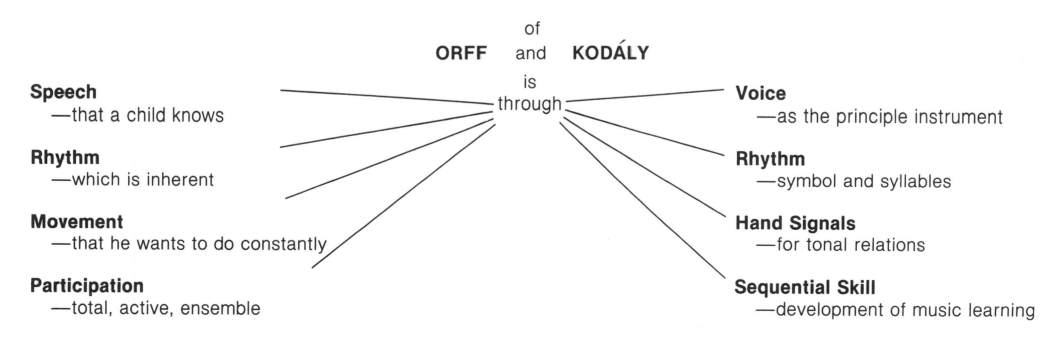

of
ORFF and **KODÁLY**
is
through

Speech
—that a child knows

Rhythm
—which is inherent

Movement
—that he wants to do constantly

Participation
—total, active, ensemble

Voice
—as the principle instrument

Rhythm
—symbol and syllables

Hand Signals
—for tonal relations

Sequential Skill
—development of music learning

Part I

This first part consists of simplified terminology and teaching techniques and suggestions that will help you.

Remember, however, that actually teaching the songs and playing the games is the most important thing.

What Is Music To A Child?

It is altogether in his
  Play-Sphere Area.

Now—About those excuses of yours . . .

Excuses, Excuses, Excuses

"But—I can't play the piano!"

Great—the children are better off without it.

"But—I can't sing!"

Yes, you can—everyone has a
"Yoo-hoo"
and that's where we start—
and where do we stop? Hopefully, nowhere!

But/and/if, you have succeeded in getting all of your first level children to sing this interval on pitch and to walk and clap a steady beat by the end of the year,

You get a GOLD STAR!

But I Don't Know My Hand Sniggles!* (Signals)

They are nothing new, but have come to us via Miss Sarah Ann Glover, England (1785–1867) with adaptations by John Curwen of England (1816–1880) and later redevelopments by Zoltán Kodály.

Why Are They Used?

To paraphrase a quote: "They are outward and visible signs of an inward and spiritual song."

Hand signals give muscular direction to leading the child's singing voice.

Do not teach these syllables by name to young children. They are to be used as an aid to the child by "seeing" pitch comparisons between the tones.

You Will Need Only Two Signals To Begin With:

Sol

Mi

For the tone of *Sol*, hold the palm of the hand about mouth level, elbow and arm out from the body. As the tone is sung, move the hand slightly out as if drawing out the sound.

For the tone of *Mi*, turn the palm down, horizontal to the floor, somewhat lower than *Sol*.
Let your whole body *feel* the intervals.

All together now: **"Yoo – Hoo!"**   **See? You're singing!**

*From Jan Morgan's second grade—Lufkin, Texas

In The Beginning—

You may want to use *Body Signals*

Why?

- they use large body movements

- they give emphasis to spacial relationship of the intervals

- when traditional hand signals are introduced, the transition is easier

- they make the activity more like a game.

How?

- for the pitch of *Sol* palms of the hands are held together in front

- for the pitch of *Mi*, palms of hands are placed flat on the lap.

NOTE: These are used in this preparation stage *just* as body motions, and syllables are not named.

There Is A Difference

Between

BEAT	and	**RHYTHM**

Beat is steady.
It can go fast or slow but
it is always steady

- as a clock
- as your pulse
- as your heartbeat

Steady beat cannot be
emphasized too strongly.

- clap it
- tap it ⎫ hands together
- pat it ⎭ on head, shoulders, desk, etc.
- walk it ⎫ alternate motions
- brush it ⎭ are more difficult, use after
                    above is secure
- feel it—put the beat "inside" you.

Rhythm is the sound of the words
in a song.

- it flows through the music
- it is movement
- it is language
- it is the lifeblood of music
- it grows out of speech patterns
- it is the heart of God
- it is the fourth "R" in learning.

Meter in Music

The notes on the music five-line *staff* are divided into "sets" called *measures*, by *bar lines*. At the beginning of the songs, there is a number, usually a *2* or a *4* that tells how many steady beats there will be in each measure. This is called the *meter*. The first beat in each measure is always the strongest, or, is *accented*.

The beats will be underlined in the majority of these songs.

The Rhythm Symbols

The notation "|" (ta, pronounced "tah") represents one sound on a steady beat.

Example: "Star   light,   star   bright"
written: | | | |
spoken: ta   ta   ta   ta

The notation "⌐¬" (ti-ti, pronounced, "tee-tee") represents a subdivision of the beat into 2 sounds.

Example: "Bee,   bee,   bum - ble   bee."
written: | | ⌐—¬ |
spoken: ta   ta   ti - ti   ta

The notation " ℥ " (rest) represents *no* sound for one beat.

Example: "Hot   cross   buns"
written: | | | ℥
spoken: ta   ta   ta   shhh (or touch lips or some other
                                                                                                motion)

The notation " ♩ " (ta - a) represents one sound held for 2 beats.

Example: "Sleep,   baby,   sleep"
written: | ⌐—¬   ♩
spoken: ta   ti - ti   ta - a

(These are the main rhythm symbols that are used in this book.)

Note: Do not write the rhythm words on the board (ta, ti - ti, etc.).

Body Percussion

Body What?

This is a term used to describe snapping the fingers, clapping the hands, patting the thighs, and stamping the feet.

Why use it?
- It involves the body in music.
- It reinforces the steady beat.
- It aids in learning to do more than one thing at a time.
- It develops auditory discrimination.
- It is a percussion instrument that is always with you.
- It is a training for using mallet instruments later.

Body Percussion Levels

There are *four levels:*

1. **Snap**   Hands held high—the little ones can't do this, but they love to try.

2. **Clap**   Teach the children to clap with one hand palm up and steady—the "instrument," while the other hand claps it with a relaxed wrist and arm, elbows out—the "mallet." This is preparation for future bar instrument playing. This position may be alternated for phrase feeling.

3. **Patschen** (potchen)   German for "leg slap." They love to say this word. Again—relaxed wrists, let the arms lift the hands.

4. **Stamp**   Bring leg back and stamp forward and down instead of raising knee and leg forward.

Examples of Body Percussion

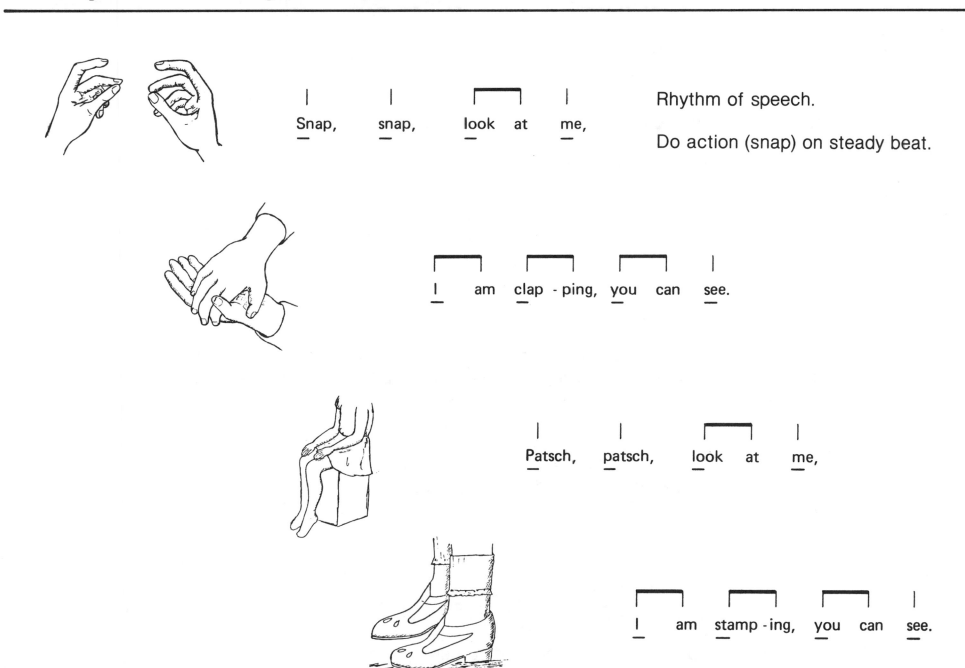

Snap, snap, look at me,

Rhythm of speech.

Do action (snap) on steady beat.

I am clap-ping, you can see.

Patsch, patsch, look at me,

I am stamp-ing, you can see.

Rhythm Echo

Using Body Percussion

Ask the children to be your "echo" and do what you do.

- Use simple 4-beat patterns—as:

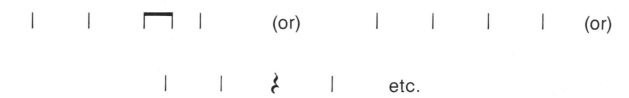

- Use only one level at a time at first, such as all *claps,* or all *patschens.* (In the beginning, do not alternate hands when doing the *patschens:* slap the thighs with both hands at the same time.)

- Next go to two levels in a descending order. It is easier for a child to go *down* than *up.*

For example: clap, clap, clap, patsch   (or) snap, snap, snap, clap

Suggestions For Song Use

"The new song is sung first in the heart—otherwise it cannot be sung at all."— *Dietrich Bonhoeffer*

Give   a background for each new musical experience to arouse interest and involve feelings.

"Do you like to play on a seesaw? Could you seesaw by yourself? Could you seesaw with an elephant?" . . .

Sing   a new song completely through, then stop and talk about it.

Teach   by *echo*—first short sections (*phrases*) then longer ones until the children know the song.

Play   the singing game, if there is one that goes with the song.

Drop out   gradually when singing with the children so they can sing alone and not depend on you constantly.

Repeat,   repeat, repeat. They do not tire of a well-loved song.

Emphasize   the steady beat—clap it, pat it, etc.

(Suggestions for Song Use continued on next page.)

NOTE: Three and four year olds would not need to go beyond this point.

Song Use, cont.

Clap   the *sounds* of the words—using two fingers of one hand clapping in the palm of the others.

Do this first while singing.

Later eliminate the words. "Lock them up in your brain."

You will be clapping the *rhythm* of the song.
Ask: "Did you hear the song inside you?"

Sing   the song again, quietly clapping the "words" on their hands.

NOTE: If they have been playing a game or activity with the song, this is an excellent way to return to their places.

Review   T. "What song am I clapping on my hands?" (Use same song.)

see - saw,   up and down,   in the air and on the ground

T. "Which words of that song am I clapping?"

Clap words in sequence parts:

then

T. "If I clap the words of the first part of the song, can you clap what comes next?"

Visual And Kinetic Reinforcement Of A Song

To aid the child in discovering that beats are steady, and that there can be *one, more than one,* or *no* sounds on a beat, use empty baby food jars for the *beats,* and sticks for the *rhythm.* You may want to put a heart on each jar to represent "heartbeats."

The child sings the song and touches each jar on the steady beat. He then decides how many sounds were sung on each beat, and puts the number of corresponding sticks in each. The empty jar represents the "rest" (𝄽).

Example:

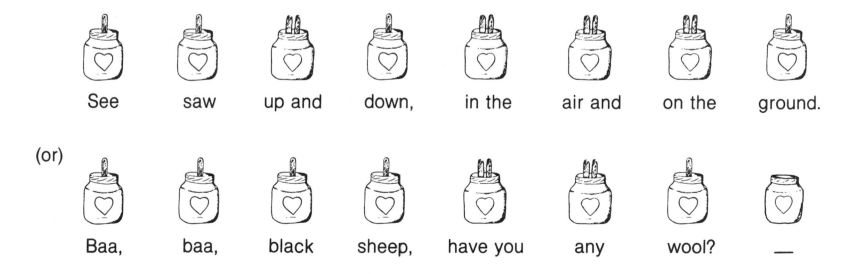

See	saw	up and	down,	in the	air and	on the	ground.

(or)

Baa,	baa,	black	sheep,	have you	any	wool?	___

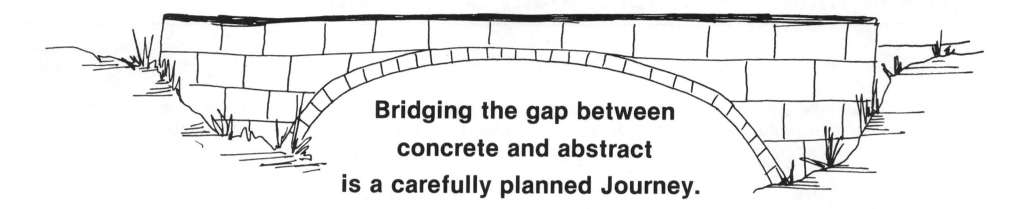

**Bridging the gap between
concrete and abstract
is a carefully planned Journey.**

Later—the symbolism of the manipulative objects can be shown by drawing hearts on the chalkboard.

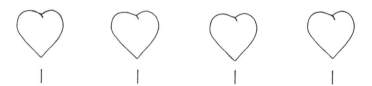

- **Point** to each one as a song is sung.

- **Write** a "ta" symbol under each heartbeat as the song is sung.

This can be named aurally at this point.

- **Practice** writing a symbol for heartbeats of the song.

NOTE: Beats may also be shown as short horizontal marks: — — — —

Kindergarten children may be taught how to do this.

"The child learns only what he discovers himself."

Written symbolism of the *divided beat* (⌐¬) and the *silent beat* (𝄽)

More than one sound to a beat:

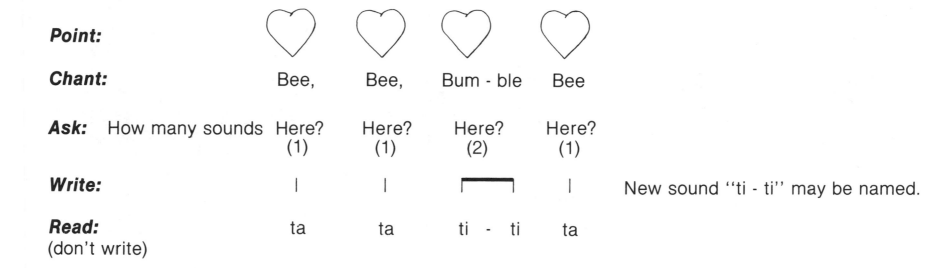

Point:	♡	♡	♡	♡
Chant:	Bee,	Bee,	Bum - ble	Bee
Ask: How many sounds	Here? (1)	Here? (1)	Here? (2)	Here? (1)
Write:	|	|	⌐‾‾¬	|	New sound "ti - ti" may be named.
Read: (don't write)	ta	ta	ti - ti	ta

Or there may be no sound:

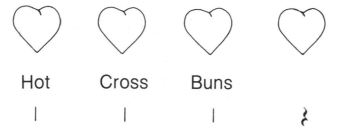

Hot   Cross   Buns

\| \| \| 𝄽

" 𝄽 " is the symbol for the silent beat, and is named a "rest."

Reinforce these skills. Use movement with children for *beat* and *rhythm*.

\| \| ⌐‾‾¬   𝄽

Concepts Of Music

The basic concepts of music are:

| loud | soft | fast | slow | up down | high | low |

These are taught through movement, rhyme, song, body percussion, singing games, etc.

Through movement a child will learn these by doing opposites:*

He learns *up* by doing *down, fast* by doing *slow, loud* by doing *soft, high* by doing *low,* etc.

*Grace Nash

Teaching Concepts, cont.*

First—*establish* a *normal,* then go from there.

    T. (normal voice) "Bee, bee, bumble bee, stung a man upon his knee.
              Stung a pig upon his snout; I declare, if you're not out."

Demonstrate a *concept* and *name* it.

    T. "I will say it again in a very soft voice."

Children will *imitate.* Don't let them whisper.

Then *demonstrate* and *name* a *contrasting concept.*

    T. "Now I will say it louder."   Do so. Children will imitate.

Refine and *develop* it.

    T. "Can you say it louder? softer? faster?," etc.
       "Can you say it in a *high* voice? a *low* voice?"
          (*High* and *low* are difficult concepts for a child to learn.)

Later—*Combine concepts:* louder and slower—softer and slower—louder and slower, etc.

*Betsy Moll

The Pentatonic Scale

(5)   **(tone)**

The majority of the songs used in this book use these 5 tones only.

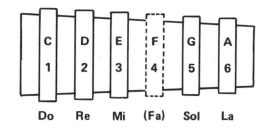

They are singing games, rhymes and folk songs that have been sung and chanted by children for generations.

They begin with two-tone (*Sol-Mi*) songs. This is a child's first natural melody.

Next, three-tone (*Sol-Mi-La*) songs are used, based on the child's natural "teasing" chant.

Do and *Re* are added next, completing the 5-tone scale that is heard in most of our folk music.

I Have A Question—

"Why do all of these songs use the same old notes over and over?"

This is to help you to learn the songs more easily. You can use your song bells that have letters and numbers on them. Once you know the song, you can, and *should*, sing it on the tones that you and the children are most comfortable with. After all, we're not all Beethovens.

A child's voice range is ordinarily between middle C and the A above, or between D and B.

"G" is a good starting pitch, and is used for "Sol," the 5th tone, in these songs. (Left alone, a child will usually sing on F♯ for the pitch of *Sol.*)

Part II

Two-Tone Songs* And Related Activities

If You Will Look To The Left

Tones Used:

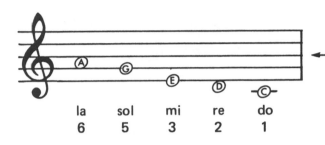

You will see that each song page is divided into two distinct secions—the song on the right and the scheme on the left. The scheme elements are explained below.

This is called the *legend.* It tells which *tones* are used in the song, also the *syllables,* the *letter names* and the *numbers* that will correspond with your song bells. The notes are arranged from the highest tone used down to the lowest.

This is the *rhythm* of the song written without the noteheads (♩) and without the staff (≣).

s   m l   s   m

These are the syllables that stand for the melody of the song. (s—Sol; m—Mi; l—La; d—Do; r—Re)

—   —   —   —

These lines show where the steady beats of the song are.

Emphasis:

This indicates use of the song in this preparation stage.

Expand/Extension:

This indicates additional activities for a more mature level of children.

Ready, Get Set—

Go on, take the plunge—

The first group of songs has only two tones. The top one is "Sol" (that's *G* or *5* on your song bells) and the bottom one is "Mi" (that's *E* or *3* on your song bells).

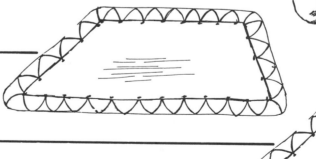

You know, there are very few things in life you can depend on, but one of them is—if *Sol* is on a line, then *Mi* is on the line below.

Ⓢ

Ⓜ

Begin The Class With Musical Greetings

Tones Used:

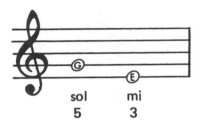

sol   mi
5   3

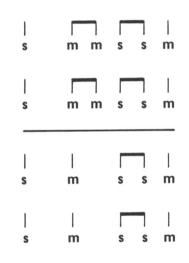

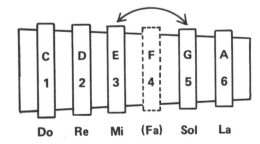

Do Re Mi (Fa) Sol La

"G" is a comfortable starting pitch. If a tuning fork is used, the pitch of "A" may be used for *Sol.*

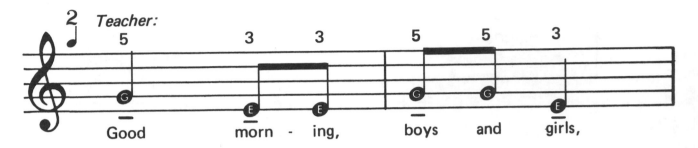

Teacher:

Good   morn - ing,   boys   and   girls,

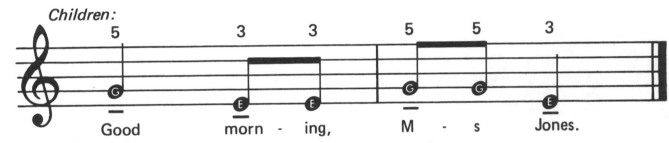

Children:

Good   morn - ing,   M - s   Jones.

Note: The steady beats are underlined.

Another Way:

Teacher:

Entering: Hel - lo,   boys   and   girls,
Leaving: Good - bye,   boys   and   girls,

Children:

Hel - lo,   M - s   Jones.
Good - bye,   M - s   Jones.

Tones Used:

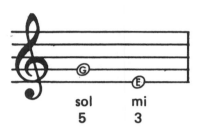

sol   mi
5   3

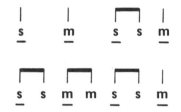

Emphasis:
- steady beat
- singing on pitch

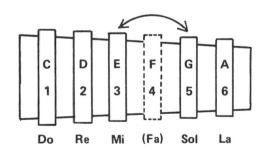

See-Saw

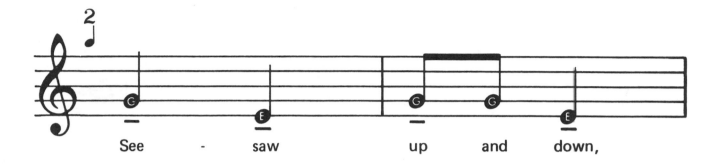

See - saw   up and down,

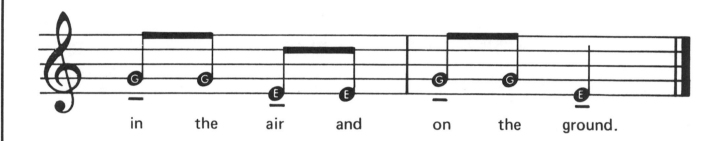

in the air and on the ground.

T: "We have something on the playground that goes like this: What is it?"

T: Sings whole song. Talk about it.
T: Sings first line. "You be my echo."
T: Sings second line. Children echo.
T: Sings whole song. Children echo.

Activity: Hold both hands with a friend, go up and down.

Extension: (Don't use with 3 and 4 year olds.) "Can you put the words on your hands?"*

*Note: Use two fingers of one hand clapping in other palm when doing this.

Movement

or, Little Bodies Out On The Floor

"Find your *space.*" They should learn to do this quickly and quietly.

- A space is where no one else is—it is your own place. No one is close enough to touch you.

- See if your arms swing freely.

Rules on the floor:

1. Never, never bump into any one.

2. Stay on your feet—don't fall down unless it's part of the game.

Comment: (You'll need it.)

"Oh, you don't understand the rules.

Please sit in the **THINKING CHAIR**
and watch the others until you are *sure* you understand, then you may go back."

Movement, cont.

Try These   *Laban/Nash*

1. How many ways can you sit in a chair?

2. "Nail" and/or "glue" your feet to the floor. How many ways can the rest of your body move now? (Un-do your feet and proceed).

3. Can you walk in a circle? A square? A triangle? (T. keeps steady beat on drum, calls out shape changes.)

4. Can you write your name in the air with your nose? Your elbow? (Expand.)

5. Can you press on the floor with your hands? Your shoulders? (Expand.)

6. Can you do karate chops in the air? (Remember our rules when out on the floor!)

7. Can you glide? Can you slide? Can you float?

8. How many ways can you punch in the air?

Starlight, Starbright

Tones used:

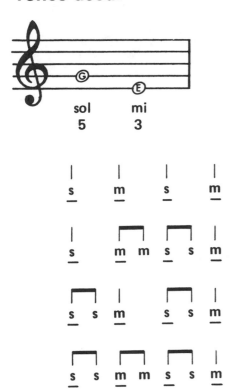

sol mi
5 3

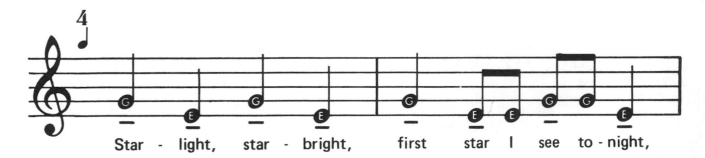

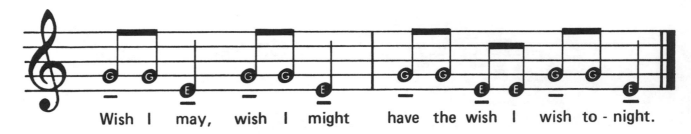

Emphasis:
- steady beat
- singing softly
- levels of *Sol* and *Mi* *

*Arm Signals: See page 13. Use only on steady beats. This is a preparation activity and syllables are not named.

Presentation:

T: Sings song through—then asks, "Have you ever made a wish?
       Did it come true?" Give children time to respond.

T: "Do you know that some people believe that if you watch for the first star
       to come out at night, then look at it over your left shoulder and sing this
       song, that your wish will come true?"

T: Sings again, using arm signals. (Note: Do not name the syllables—*Sol*
       and *Mi*. The arm signals are just motions for unconscious learning at this
       point.)

T: Sings first measure, ch. echo. T. sings second measure, ch. echo.
       T. sings third measure, ch. echo. For fourth measure combine parts, then
       sing entire song, ch. echo.

Starlight, Starbright, cont.

Extension:

If two resonator bells are available, the melody may be played by a child when song is secure.

Place them in this position:

ANOTHER DAY:

Visual Reinforcement: Use magnetic (or felt) stars on a magnetic (or felt) board to show high and low levels of the songs:

Again—use just one star for each steady beat. Sing and point. A connecting line between stars may be drawn if a magnetic board is used.

One, Two, Tie My Shoe

Tones Used:

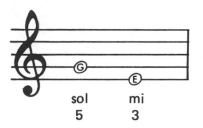

sol   mi
5   3

s m s s m

Traditional

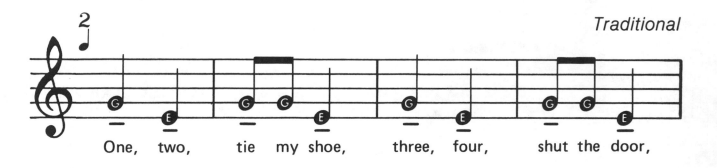

One, two, tie my shoe, three, four, shut the door,

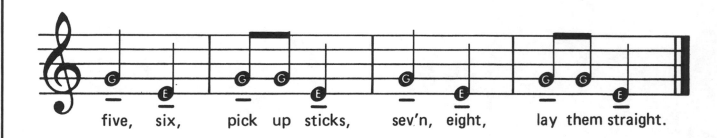

five, six, pick up sticks, sev'n, eight, lay them straight.

Emphasis:

- use of the child's natural rhythm pattern

- levels of *Sol* and *Mi* through use of body signals or beats.

- counting aid for small ones.

Continue

nine, ten, big fat hen,

'leven, twelve, dig and delve,

thirteen, fourteen, maids, a-courtin',

fifteen, sixteen, maids in the kitchen,

seventeen, eighteen, maids a-waitin',

nineteen, twenty, my plate's empty.

Rhythm changes, keep steady beat

Hey, Hey Look At Me

Traditional

Tones Used:

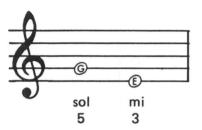

sol   mi
5   3

s m s s m

s s m m s s m

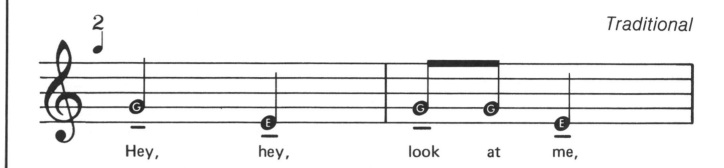

Hey,   hey,   look at me,

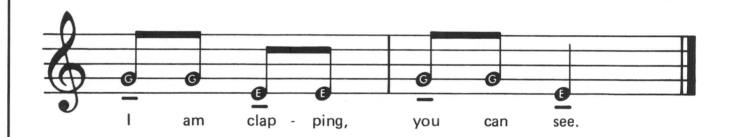

I am clap - ping, you can see.

Other actions: flying, smiling, tapping, snapping, turning, patching, singing, etc.

Another day: Clap just the rhythm of the words. Ask, "Who remembers this song?"

Extension: "Can you lock up the words in your head and put them on your hands?"

Uses:

- echo singing

- independent singing

- individual movement

Be My Mirror

Note: This activity may be correlated with "Hey, Hey, Look At Me"—i.e., "I am waving, you can see."

(Think: S-l-o-w M-o-t-i-o-n)

T. and child sit facing one another.

Show them "how"

T. has object (ball, hand puppet, etc. in one hand.
 T. moves it up, down, around, side to side, etc.
 Child follows with just eyes.

Repeat, using other hand.

Let me try it.

Let the child be the leader, T. will "eye-follow."

Extension:

Have children do this procedure in two's, taking turns being the "leader."

Note: The children will become more secure if you begin with two, then each of these will choose a new partner to "teach;" continue until all are participating.

This allows time for observation and peer evaluation.

Be My Mirror, cont.

(Use eye-contact here)

Go Slowly!

T. Does "cool wave" using one hand.
   (Palm up facing partner—rotate slowly, first one way, then the other.)

Child is your "mirror"—does the same thing with the hand on the same side.

Repeat with other hand. Do not touch.

(Variation of same procedure: Wave "Good-bye," be a windshield wiper, etc.)

Another day!

Let child be the leader with T.

Do with other partners.

Same procedure using one foot, then one foot and one hand.

Be careful! If problems occur here, back up.

Next—use both hands at once, first both in one direction with same motion, then repeat in opposite direction. Then have each hand do something different. Try one hand and one foot.

Graduation!

Be a Super-Smarty—use elbows, eyebrows, knees, nose, shoulders, head, hips, . . .

Quaker, Quaker

Tones Used:

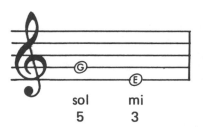

sol   mi
5   3

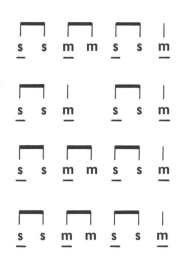

s s m m s s m

s s m s s m

s s m m s s m

s s m m s s m

Emphasis:
- question/answer
- game
- individual singing
- steady beat
- arm signals

Traditional

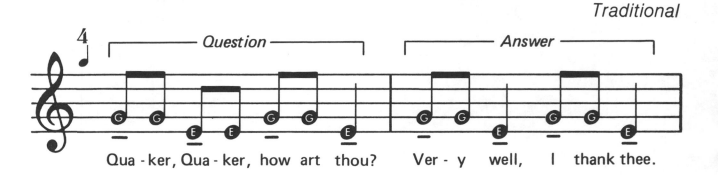

Qua - ker, Qua - ker, how art thou?   Ver - y well, I thank thee.

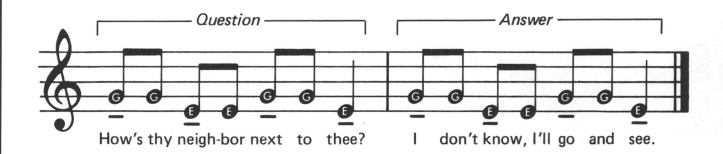

How's thy neigh-bor next to thee?   I don't know, I'll go and see.

Background: T. explain words of song. Teach by rote. (See "See-Saw".)

Game: Two circles, inner one facing out to partner. Outside circle sings question part, inner circle answers. Then all go step-close to the right, clap hands twice, and repeat the song until back to original partner.

For Variety: Switch Q. and A. parts. Also, arm signals may be used on underlined steady beats. (Palms together for *Sol,* to knees for *Mi*)

Also, for individual singing: Double up fist, let thumb be the "puppet" for a child to sing to his neighbor, who answers, then turns to his neighbor and repeats, etc.

In And Out

Counting-out Rhyme

Tones Used:

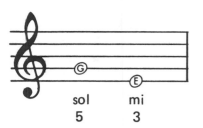

sol   mi
5   3

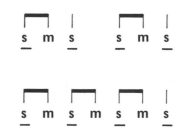

s m s   s m s

s m s m s m s

Emphasis:

- steady beat
- physical experience of *in* and *out*

Extension:

One child may play the tone "G" on the steady beats.

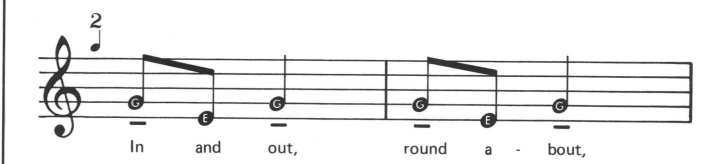

In   and   out,   round   a   -   bout,

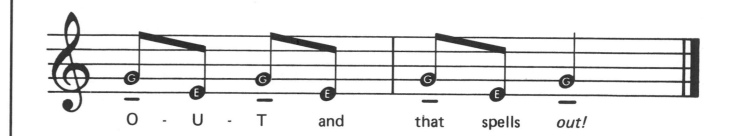

O   -   U   -   T   and   that   spells   *out!*

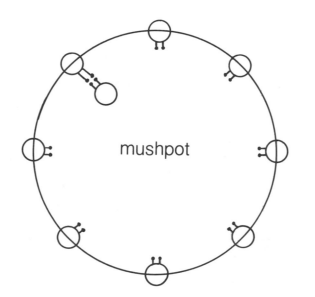

mushpot

Game:

Circle formation, all stand with both fists held to their chests.

Leader in circle pulls one person's fists *in,* then *pushes* them back (out), steps to the next person, repeats, then to the next, repeats, and the fourth one he comes to will either be in the "mushpot," or he may change places with the leader.

Pease Porridge Hot

Chant

Emphasis:

- steady beat
- preparation for the rest (𝄽)

1. Pease por-ridge hot, *(Blow on porridge to cool it)* pease por-ridge cold, *(Make "B-r-r-r" sound, or say "Yuk!")*
2. Some like it hot, some like it cold,

Pease por-ridge in the pot, nine days old. *(Pick up "bowl" [cupped hands] as if sniffing, say "Phew!")*
Some like it in the pot, nine days old.

T. Who knows what porridge is? Children respond.
T. I know a rhyme about some porridge that probably didn't taste too good. Listen, then tell me why.

Activity:

- Teach by rote to children.

Extension:

- Have them clap on the rests.
- Have them walk the beat, say the rhyme, and turn to walk in another direction on the claps.

Remember—we never, never bump.

Note:

"Pease" is an old plural for "pea."

"Porridge" is a cereal cooked to a thick consistency. (A British word.)

Red Light—Green Light

A Safety Rhythm

pt = patschen   *cl* = clap   *st* = stamp   (Steady beats in the rhythm are underlined.)

| Red | light, | green | light, | yel - low | in be - tween; | |
| cl | pt | cl | pt | cl | pt cl | pt |

| Be | care - ful, | be | safe, | find out | what they mean. | |
| cl | pt | cl | pt | cl | pt cl | pt |

| "Stop," | says | Red, | | "Go," | says | Green, | |
| st | cl | cl | | st | cl | cl | |

| "Wait," | says | Yel - low, please be | care - ful | in be - tween. | |
| st | cl | cl cl | cl | cl cl | |

Use with: "Stop, Look, And Listen," Grace Nash *Music With Children*, Series I

Stop, Look, And Listen

Grace Nash
Music With Children, Series I
used with permission

Tones Used:

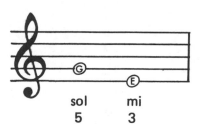

sol   mi
5   3

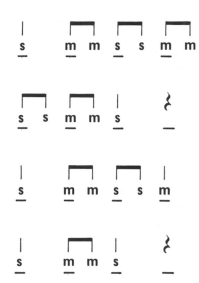

(spoken)

1. Stop, look and lis - ten,   be - fore you cross the street. (WAIT!)
2. Wait for the light to change be - fore you cross the street. (WAIT!)

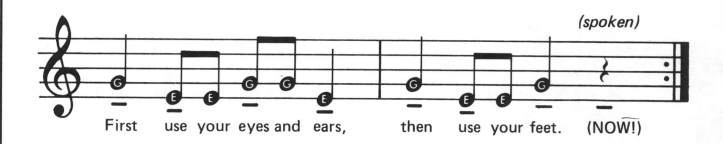

(spoken)

First   use your eyes and ears,   then   use your feet.   (NOW!)

Children should dramatize this.

Emphasis:

- combine safety consciousness with music.

One child, the "safety patrol person" or the "traffic cop," could sing to the others before they "cross the street," a designated area in the room.

Tinker-Tailor

Traditional

Tones Used:

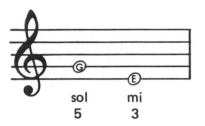

sol   mi
5   3

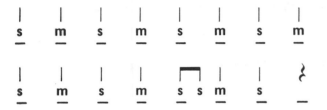

s m s m s m s m

s m s m s s m s

Suggested Extension and Form:

1. Add a few rhythm instruments to play on the beat (see above music). No singing—use inner hearing.
2. Continue instruments, add low notes of C and G (play at same time) for duration of song.
3. Continue all above, add song.
4. Continue instruments and song, have one child play melody on G and E bells.
5. All stop—8 children each say a word name using "funny voices" on beat. End with gong or cymbal crash.

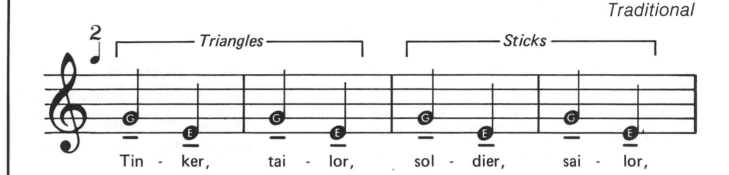

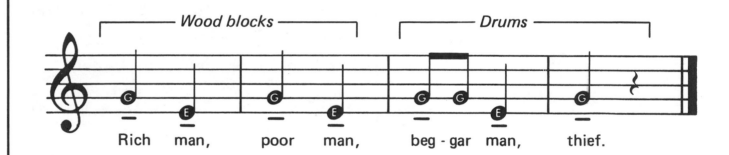

1. T. sings song to children. Discuss words.

2. Count buttons on several children while singing to see "what they will be when they grow up."

3. Use as counting-out rhyme to see who will be "it" or leader for next game. Point or touch each child on steady beat.

4. To use as a performance number, first sing the song, then follow procedure on the left.

I Have A Cat

Speech Rondo

Rondo Form

Wilma Salzman
used with permission

A B A C A D A etc.

A rondo is a form in which a section is sung, played, clapped, or spoken (A). Then a different part is performed (B), then the first part repeated (A) then a new part (C), etc.

Some refer to a rondo as "Dagwood sandwich."

A. T. "I have a cat." (Form whiskers with hands crossed over face, fingers spread apart. Children *echo.*)

B. T. "My cat is fat." (Make fat stomach with two arms. Ch. *echo.*)

A. T. Repeat "I have a cat . . ."

C. T. "My cat wears a hat." (Form hat with hands. Ch. *echo.*)

A. T. Repeat "I have a cat . . ."

D. T. "My cat caught a bat." (Form wings with hands. Ch. *echo.*)

A. T. Repeat "I have a cat . . ."

E. T. "My cat says, 'Meow!' (Ch. *echo.*)

Extensions: Clap the rhythm of the words while doing speech.

Later, drop the words, clap the rhythm only. Use *echo* process first.

Later, let the children clap the "A" sections, T. or others clap other parts.

Make up a story about a dog. Use voice inflections, add "woof!" at the end.

Sesame Street

(Orff Demonstration)

**by Linda Morgan
and Nancy Ferguson**
used with permission

Tones Used:

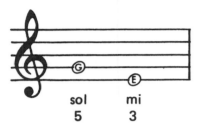

sol   mi
5   3

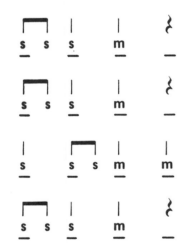

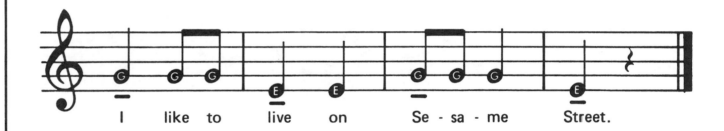

Emphasis:

- rondo (see page 48)
- movement
- dramatization
- arm levels of tones

Activity: Introduction—Chant in a "dark" voice: Big bird, big bird
Children take large steps, flop wings with each step.

A. *Sing* the song, move freely, use *Sol* and *Mi* arm signals on underlined words. (For level movement only.)

B. *Chant* (monster voice—shrug shoulders up and down alternately):

"Cook - ie   mon - ster   eats   my   cook - ies"

A. *Sing* with arm signals.

C. *Chant* (sqeaky voice—raise garbage can lid up and down):

"Os - car's   in   the   gar - bage   can"

A. *Sing*—then repeat introduction for the ending (coda).

Three Tone Songs* And Related Activities

You Did Great On Two Tones—

Would you like to try for three?

"La" is a curious fellow—he stays close to "Sol," so he can *lean* over and see what's going on. He is not a copy-cat like "Sol" and "Mi" who always have to be either both line notes or both space notes—he wants to be different: if "Sol" and "Mi" are line notes, he is in the space above "Sol." If "Sol" and "Mi" move to spaces, he goes to the line above "Sol."

In these next songs, we will use these three tones. "La" is *A* or *6* on your bells.

La

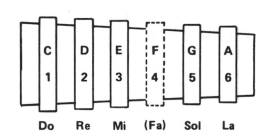

Note: Pre-school children don't need to know all of this. Just let them sing the songs and play the games.

Bounce High, Bounce Low

Tones Used:

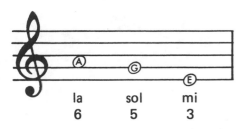

la   sol   mi
6   5   3

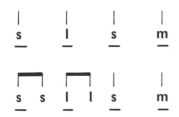

Emphasis:
- steady beat
- phrasing
- aural preparation of tone *La* close to *Sol.*

Correlated Movement:
- Ball is on the floor. Have different children move it around in a small circle with their toe, heel, elbow, nose.

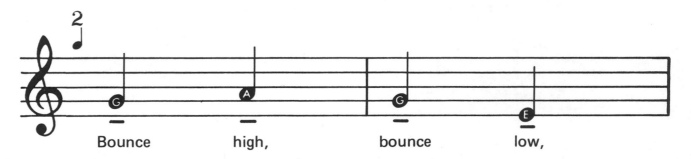

Bounce   high,   bounce   low,

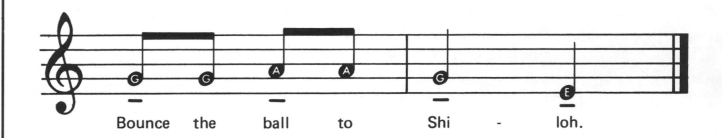

Bounce   the   ball   to   Shi - loh.

Activity: T. bounces ball to each child in circle formation. (Think: bounce, catch, bounce, catch.) If a child bounces ball too high, just say, ''Oh, you didn't understand, let me give you another try.'' This usually does it.

Later: Have 4 children stand in square formation, bounce and catch to song around the square. They will discover that it is back to the first person at the end of the song. This is development of a feeling for phrases.

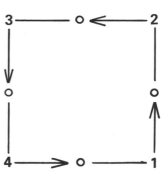

Plainsies, Clapsies

Ball Activity

from Tom Kite*

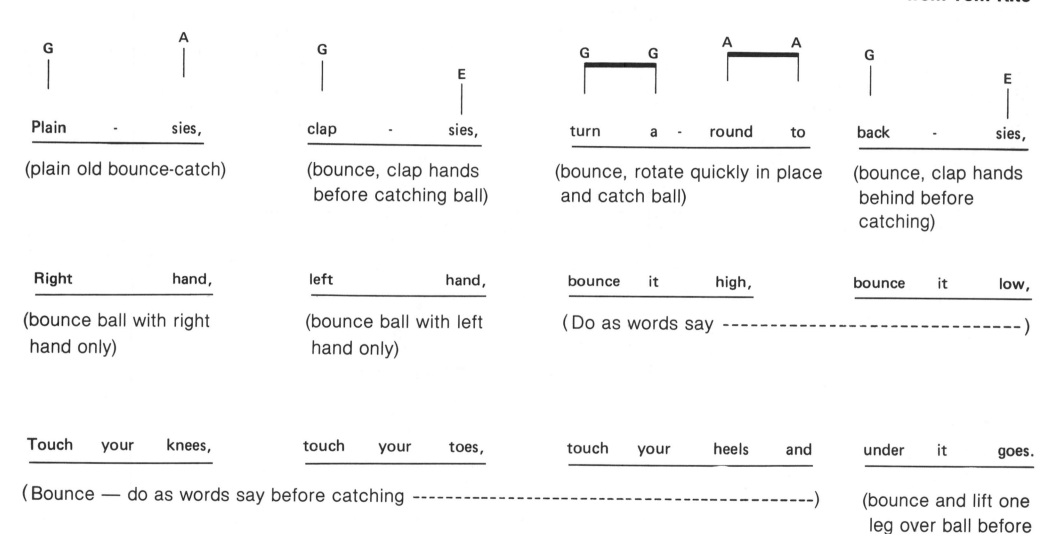

G   A

Plain - sies,

(plain old bounce-catch)

G   E

clap - sies,

(bounce, clap hands before catching ball)

G G   A   A

turn a - round to

(bounce, rotate quickly in place and catch ball)

G   E

back - sies,

(bounce, clap hands behind before catching)

Right hand,

(bounce ball with right hand only)

left hand,

(bounce ball with left hand only)

bounce it high,

(Do as words say ------------------------------)

bounce it low,

Touch your knees,

touch your toes,

touch your heels and

under it goes.

(Bounce — do as words say before catching ---)

(bounce and lift one leg over ball before catching)

Emphasis:

- delighted children
- exhausted teacher

collected by Tom Alvord
used with permission

Doggie, Doggie, Where's Your Bone?

Tones Used:

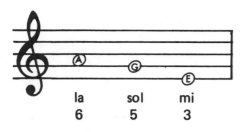

la sol mi
6 5 3

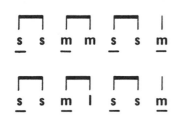

s s m m s s m

s s m l s s m

Emphasis:

- game
- use of *La* only once
- aural discrimination

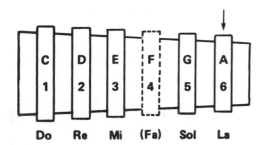

Do Re Mi (Fa) Sol La
1 2 3 4 5 6

Traditional

Dog - gie, dog - gie, where's your bone?

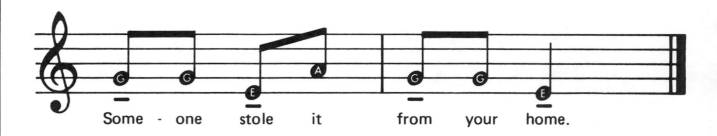

Some - one stole it from your home.

Dog: (spoken) **Who stole my bone?**

Answer: Arf, arf. (or) Orff, orff?

Game: "Doggie" is asleep, either in front of room, or in center of circle. A "bone" (eraser) is by his side. T. indicates one child to tiptoe up and get the bone, return to his place and hide it behind him.

Class sings song—Doggie asks question (no peekie!)—Bone-burglar barks. Then doggie turns around, eyes open, and has 3 guesses as to who-done-it. Right or wrong, the bone-swiper is the new doggie, and the old dog gets to choose the next bone-swiper. And on—and on—and . . . .

Sounds Of Your VOICE

(Choristers Guild)

Helen Kemp
used with permission

T. "This is my whispering voice."
(children echo.)

T. "This is my speaking voice."
(children echo.)

T. "This is my shouting voice!"
(children echo.)

sol sol sol sol sol
T. "This is my singing   mi
                       voice."
(children echo.)

NOTE: This is a good voice reminder, especially when they forget to leave their "outside voices" on the playground.

Lucy Locket

Tones Used:

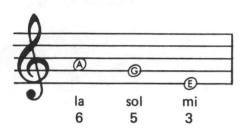

la   sol   mi
6   5   3

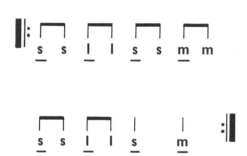

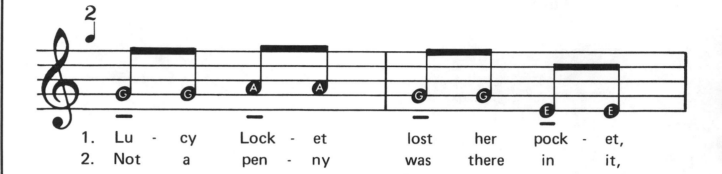

1. Lu - cy Lock - et lost her pock - et,
2. Not a pen - ny was there in it,

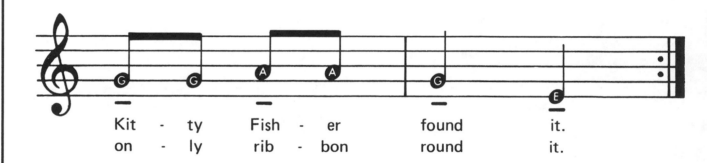

Kit - ty Fish - er found it.
on - ly rib - bon round it.

T. sings song: Give "story background," i.e. "*pocket*" means purse or pocketbook, where Lucy was when she lost it, how she felt, where Kitty Fisher found it, what Lucy said when Kitty returned it, etc.
Teach by rote.

Emphasis:

- concept of loud-soft (dynamics)

- preparation for teaching repeat sign later.

Game: One child is "it," goes to corner, hides eyes. T. gives "pocket" (eraser, etc.) to a child who puts it behind him. All hands are behind backs. On ready signal ('Ready, Freddie!' "it" walks slowly around the room. Others sing *softly* if "it" is *not* close to "pocket," gradually singing *louder* as "it" gets closer, and *loud* (don't shout!) when beside person with pocket. Person who had object is new "it," and first "it" gives pocket to someone else. Continue ad infinitum.

Movement for  Concept

Dalcroze demonstration

T. Use hand drum. If class is large, first demonstrate with six or eight children, then add other circles.

1. Children stand in small circle holding hands; stand close.
   Begin soft drum beat, keep it *steady*.
   Ch. begin walking to the beat (in small steps) to the left.

2. As drum tone gradually becomes louder (but *not* faster),
   Ch. enlarge their steps and extend their arms to sound of the drum.

3. As drum tone becomes softer, circle closes in.

4. Continue, going from soft (small steps, close together) to loud (large steps, arms extended).

5. Later: to keep children from automatically going in and out, vary length of drum tone.

Mill Wheel

Tones Used:

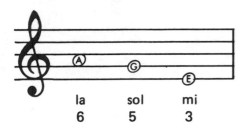

la sol mi
6   5   3

Emphasis:
- feeling of higher pitch of "la"
- feeling of silent beat.

Game:

Ch. form a circle by two's and walk to the steady beat while one child—the "Miller"—stands in the center. At end of song he calls out, "FLOUR!" All change partners quickly—and the miller tries to get one, too. Child left out becomes new "miller."

Extension: Sing while drawing a wheel on chalkboard to each beat. "Squirt" the oil on the silent beat (𝄽).

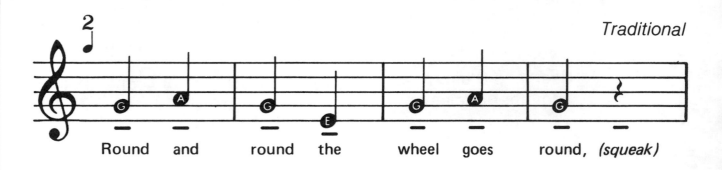

Round and round the wheel goes round, *(squeak)*

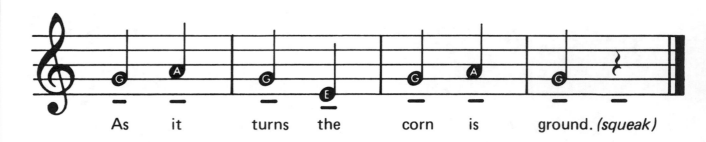

As it turns the corn is ground. *(squeak)*

Discuss a Mill Wheel for background—its use, size, etc.

T. I know a song about a Mill Wheel. I will sing it to you. Do you think I will sing it fast or slow? (Discuss)

T. Sings song. Teach by rote—"Can you show me with your hand how the wheel goes around?"

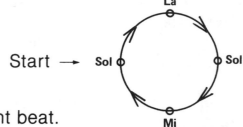

Say: "Squeak" on silent beat.

T. "Let's oil that squeak and see if that sound goes away." Sing—omit squeak.

Clap With Me!

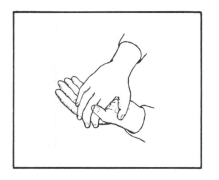

Remember how to clap! One hand is flat—palm up. The other hand claps with a relaxed wrist. Hold arms and elbows slightly out from the body. Bounce a little!

Switch hands occasionally! Get the feeling all over you!

T. "As soon as you see what I'm doing, join in." (Don't tell)

1. **Concepts:** Begin at a medium rate of speed and a medium sound, then clap *louder, softer* (for dynamics)—*faster, slower* (for tempo). Clap with hands close to floor, then raise high to show levels—do not get loud or soft here.

   Later extension: loud and slow; soft and slow; loud and fast; soft and fast.
   Ask: "What did I do?"

2. **Catch me:** Clap a simple rhythm, children join as soon as they catch on. When *all* are clapping, change the pattern without stopping. Continue. Examples of patterns:

Bell Horses

Tones Used:

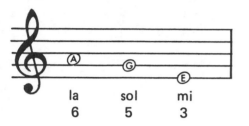

la sol mi
6 5 3

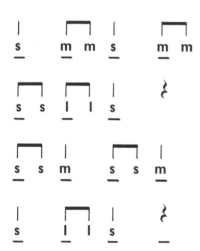

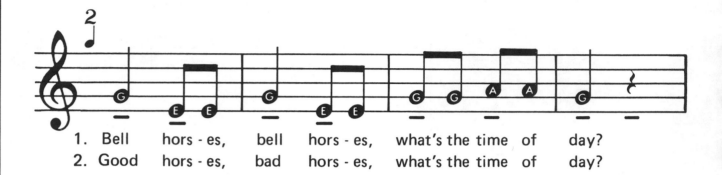

2

1. Bell hors - es, bell hors - es, what's the time of day?
2. Good hors - es, bad hors - es, what's the time of day?

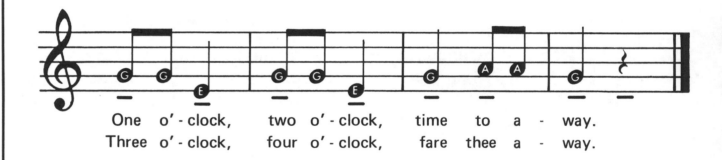

One o' - clock, two o' - clock, time to a - way.
Three o' - clock, four o' - clock, fare thee a - way.

This is an excellent number to use for performance or demonstration. The children will experience the satisfaction of musically building up a number from an *Introduction* (the "clock" striking four) to the full song and movement, and ending with a *Coda* (the horse whinny and "whoa").

Emphasis:

- steady beat
- inner hearing
- improvisation
- dramatization
- instrument playing

Instruments needed:

1. Gong or cymbal for clock sound.
2. Wood blocks, coconut shells, or styrofoam cups for "clip-clop."
3. Jingle bells.

Bell Horses, cont.

Suggested Procedure:

1. *Gong*—four beats (pause)

2. Begin *clip-clop* sounds for 8 beats—then add . . .

3. *Wrist Bells*—either on steady beat with the clip-clop, or faster in a rhythm; then begin.

4. *Song*—first verse—and *movement:*

   Groups of 3 children holding hands in △ formation, one facing outward (the "lead" horse). All trot during song.

5. *Interlude*—think the words, and "paw the ground" while clip-clops and bells play 16 beats.

6. *Song*—second verse and movement.

7. *Clip-clops* and *bells* play for 8 beats, then bells stop, clip-clops play 8 more beats, stop.

   All horses "whinny," others say "WHOA!"

Ah! Color!

Movement and Voice Inflection:

yellow yellow yellow yellow
(bounce)

RED RED RED RED
(jabbing chops)

PURPLE
(majestic)

orange
(arm sweeps)

BLUE
(glide—sway)

green
(sustained)

Let the children discuss how different colors make them feel.

As they move to color names, have them speak the word with their movement using voice inflections.

Later, divide up in groups, have a "director" to indicate when they are to perform. He may use one at a time, or combine two or more contrasting ones.

Call your production "Sunset."

And More Color!

Rainbow colors. Tune: "Ten Little Indians"

1. "Seven colors are in the rainbow, (sing 3 times)
   Seven can be seen."

2. "Red and orange and yellow and green, (sing 3 times)
   blue, indigo, and violet."

> **Secret** (Don't tell) How to remember the rainbow colors in sequence: They spell a man's name: ROY G. BIV

Use color names to dismiss the children. (Use drum on underlined steady beat.)

If you're wearing something pink ___ then you may go. ___ ___ ___ ___

If you're wearing something orange ___ then you may go. ___ ___ ___ ___

If you're wearing something yellow ___ then you may go. ___ ___ ___ ___

Continue: green, purple, red, blue, black, brown, white

Tip: Don't begin with a prominent color such as *Blue* or *Brown,* or you will have a pile-up at the door!

We Are Dancing In the Forest

Tones Used:

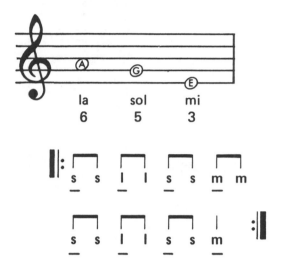

la   sol   mi
6   5   3

s s l l s s m m

s s l l s s m

Emphasis:
- fun game
- language
- feeling for repeat
- comparison of familiar song ("Lucy Locket")

T. sings to "loo." "Do you know another song that sounds like this?"

Later: T. sings first line to "loo"—then second line.
Then ask: "What did you notice?"

(Just alike) T. Yes, I *repeated* the first part.

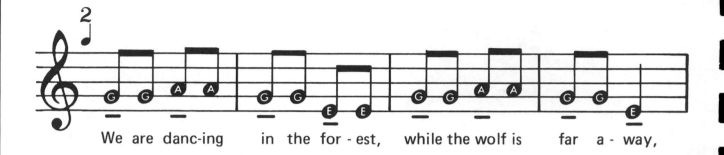

We are danc-ing in the for-est, while the wolf is far a-way,

Who knows what will hap-pen to us, if he finds us at our play.

Game:
(First designate a "home" for children to run to, and a place for wolf to live.) Children (use 6 or 8 in each group) dance about singing song. At end of song they cup their hands and call, "Wolf, what are you doing?" Wolf answers, "I'm putting on my shoes," or "I'm brushing my teeth," etc. They repeat song and dance and question wolf again. The third time he says, "I'm putting in my teeth." He tags someone, then there are 2 wolves, then 4, then 8, etc.

Alternate Game:
(Quieter and better for smaller spaces.) All children are in circle formation, and walk clockwise to the steady beat while singing. They stop at the end of the song and proceed as above on question and answer to wolf. Continue until the third time. At this point the children FREEZE with eyes tightly closed. The wolf then tiptoes around the outside circle, grabs someone from the rear and says, "Gotcha!" That person becomes the wolf.

Ostinato

(Tune: "Are You Sleeping")

"Ostinato, ostinato. What are you? What are you? What are you?

I'm a little pattern. I'm a little pattern.

Stubborn, too. Stubborn, too."*

An ostinato is a short rhythmic pattern that is repeated through speech, body percussion, song, or instrument playing.

Example:

One group chants and claps (or patschen)   while **another group** sings:

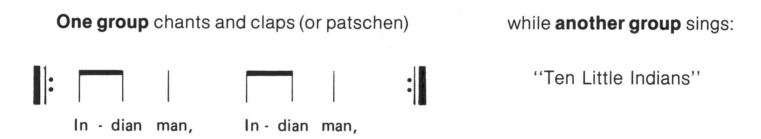

In - dian man,   In - dian man,   "Ten Little Indians"

There are many extensions and variations of ostinati, but go slowly. For example, later the children could clap the ostinato and sing the song at the same time.

*Murray G. McNair—*used with permission*

Rain, Rain, Go Away

Tones Used:

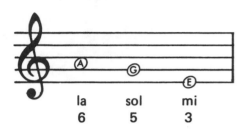

la   sol   mi
6   5   3

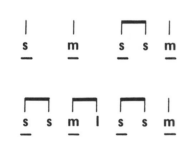

```
|   |   ⌐||   |
s   m   s  s   m

⌐|⌐  ⌐|   ⌐|⌐  |
s  s  m  l   s  s   m
```

Emphasis:

- steady beat
- language development of sound words
- ostinato

Extension (for later development):

- drawings to show beat
- writing rhythm symbols to show how many sounds on each beat.

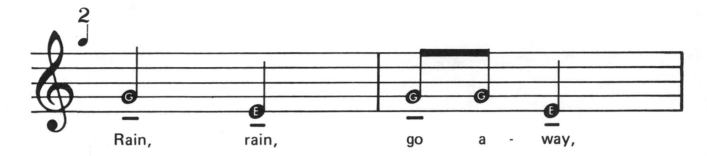

Rain,   rain,   go a - way,

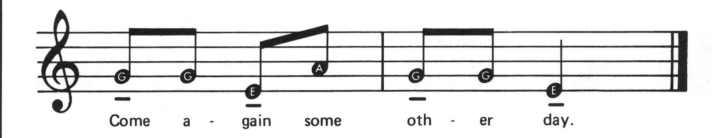

Come a - gain some   oth - er   day.

T. ''We need the rain to make things grow but why did it have to rain today? Perhaps if we sing to it, it might go away.''

T.   Sings—Children echo.

T. ''Did it work? Or is it still raining? If it is, we'll just have fun with the sounds of the rain.''
    (Discuss: pitter-patter, drip-drop, splish-splash.)

Activity: Ostinati

One group begins: ‖: ⌐|| ⌐|| ⌐|| ⌐|| :‖ patschen and chant
                      pit - ter pat - ter pit - ter pat - ter

After 8 beats, add another: ‖: | | | | :‖ clap and chant
                               drip drop drip drop

After 8 beats, add a song.

Rain, Rain, Go Away, cont.

T. and children sing song, T. draws umbrellas on steady beat:

T. sings slowly, touches each drawing using rhythm of the words
(one sound, one touch; two sounds, two touches).

Repeat, and ask on each beat, "How many sounds did you hear on this beat?"

Answer: "One." T. makes "ta" mark under drawing:

Continue through song. **Note:** on third beat, two sounds are heard.

Mark it: —name it "ti-ti.

Later: For visual of *Rhythm* and *High-Low* intervals —all sing while
T. draws. (May use 3 colors of chalk.)*

*Activity: Charlene Watson

HAPPINESS

(Speech, Body Percussion, Instruments)   **arr. by A. A. Milne**

John had great big waterproof boots on.

John had a great big waterproof hat.

John had a great big waterproof mackintosh.

"And that," said John, "Is that."

T. "I know a boy named John who didn't mind the rain because he had so many
waterproof things on."

(Discuss "waterproof.")

T. "Listen while I tell you about him, and when I get through, tell me all of the
waterproof things he had on."

T. says poem. Discuss words.

Teach poem by rote, echoing lines.

NOTE: Although the Orff extension on the following page is too difficult for early
childhood, it is included here in order that the possibilities of sound and instrument
exploration may be seen by the teacher.

And More HAPPINESS

Orff demonstration

T. This time when we say the poem, each time we say the name *John*, we will stamp our foot.

The next time—*stamp* on the word *John,* and *patschen* when we say *great big.*

Third time—do above, and *clap* when we say *waterproof (fill-in).*

Fourth time—do all of above, and *snap* when we say *that.*

Extension: First do as above, then do just the *body percussion,* leaving out the *words.*

Also: Instruments could be added in addition to the body percussion as:

Drum—for *John*
Tambourine—for *great big*
Wood block—for *waterproof (fill-in)*
Triangle—for *that*

Four-Tone Songs* and Related Activities

This section is for the preparation of the syllable *Do.*

Do is the home tone of a song.

The place of *Do* in the song is said to be the *key.*

The hand signal
for *Do* is a fist.

The arm signal is
a fist by the side of
the knees.

The following illustration is appealing to children, and can be made into a permanent wall display, beginning with just two houses, *Sol* and *Mi,* and adding the others as needed.

New Neighbors In Town

This is a *slowly* (please!) growing housing development. For weeks there were only two occupants—*Sol* and *Mi*. Of course *Mi* had to build a house just like *Sol's*, only down the street on the other side of that vacant lot. Then nosy neighbor *La* had to build close to *Sol* so he could lean over and hear what the latest news was. And one morning, he heard it!

s	m	s	s s m.	m	s s s	m m m m	s m d
Ho!	Ho!	What	do you know!	We	have a new	neigh-bor and his	name is *Do.*

Now, because *Do* lives in the first house at the bottom of the hill, and because his voice sounds rather important, the others named him Mayor, and gave *Do* the keys to the city.

Re moved in sometime later, just slid in the back door quietly. Although the others have seen him and heard him, no one has met him yet.

Oh, well, later on . . . .

Ring Around The Rosy

Tones Used:

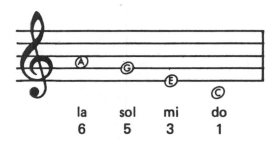

la	sol	mi	do
6	5	3	1

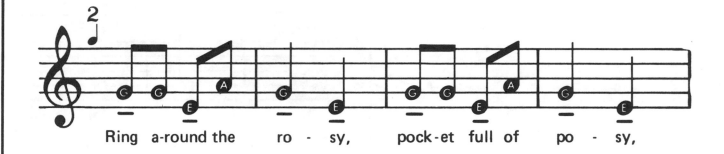

Ring a-round the ro - sy, pock-et full of po - sy,

Ash - es, ash - es, all fall down.

Emphasis:

- game
- preparation for "Do"
- preparation for half note

  ♩ (ta-a)

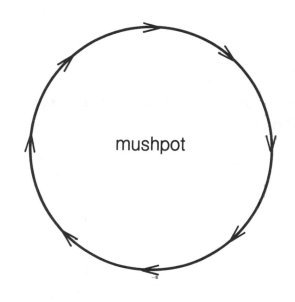

mushpot

- circle game
- children sing and circle to the left
- may or may not hold hands
- on last word, all fall down
- last one to go down goes in the mushpot
- when new one goes in mushpot, old one goes out

Fuzzy Wuzzy

Tones Used:

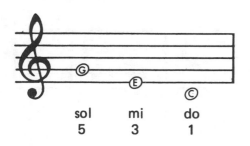

sol   mi   do
5   3   1

Emphasis

- preparation for syllable *Do*
- spoken words in a song

Extension

"The Bear Went over the Mountain."

- feeling for *accent*

T. "Would you like to step on a bear?"

- *chant* (or sing traditional tune)
- *walk* on steady beat, step hard on words "bear" and "see"

Second verse—step on "other" and "see."

Super-Smarty Extensions:

Walk the beat, *step* the accent, *clap* the rhythm, *change directions* on the phrases.

Fuz-zy Wuz-zy was a bear, Fuz-zy Wuz-zy had no hair.

(spoken)

Fuz-zy Wuz-zy was-n't fuz-zy, was he? *WELL, WAS HE?*

A fun song!

Let them rap the floor or the sides of their chairs on words "was a bear" and "had no hair."

Use a doubled fist—this is preparation for later using this hand signal for *Do.*

Page's Train

Tones Used:

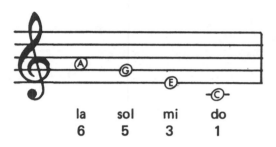

la	sol	mi	do
6	5	3	1

𝄐 —half note, two beats

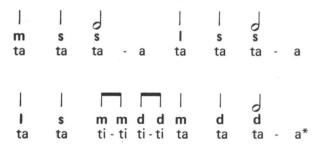

m	s	s		s	s
ta	ta	ta - a	ta	ta	ta - a

l	s	m m d d m	d	d
ta	ta	ti-ti ti-ti ta	ta	ta - a*

Emphasis:

- fast-slow beats
- feeling for ta-a (𝄐 —half note) phrasing

*For prep. use only—don't write

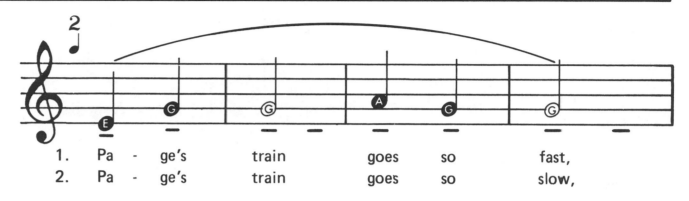

1. Pa - ge's train goes so fast,
2. Pa - ge's train goes so slow,

Can't see noth-ing but the win - dow glass.
Takes so long to get to Buf - fa - lo.

Movement with song: Elbows bent and fists doubled. Alternate back and forth on steady beat (underlined) fast—then slow.

T. "Page's train has four tunnels to go through. Please sing while I draw them." Then: "Please sing again while I make a mark for each choo of the train"

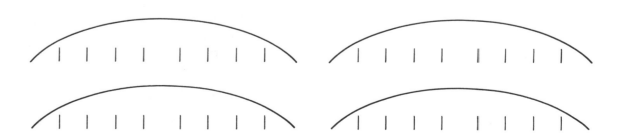

Engine, Engine, Number Nine

Emphasis:

- steady beat
- fast, slow
- loud, soft
- ostinato (A repeated pattern that is performed at the same time as the chant.)

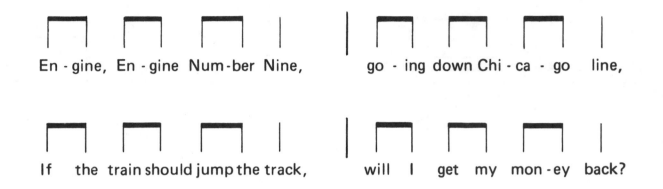

En - gine, En - gine Num - ber Nine,   go - ing down Chi - ca - go line,

If   the train should jump the track,   will I get my mon - ey back?

Extension:

- aural discrimination

Help the children discover that all four rhythm patterns are the same.

Suggested Movement: Use doubled fists and bent elbows alternating back and forth to show steady beat.

T. (after chant is learned) Establish a normal, then go to contrasts from there.

> "How would the train sound if it were closer than this?
> "How would the train sound if it were far down the track?"
> "Can you make the train go faster than this?"
> "Can you make the train go slower than this?"

Activity: *Railway Sidecar* Two children sit facing each other on floor, feet touching, holding hands, knees slightly bent. As one child leans forward, the other leans backward. Rock back and forth to show steady beat of the song.

Add ostinato:

choo,   choo,   choo-choo train

Little Sally Water

Tones Used:

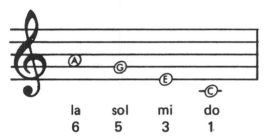

la	sol	mi	do
6	5	3	1

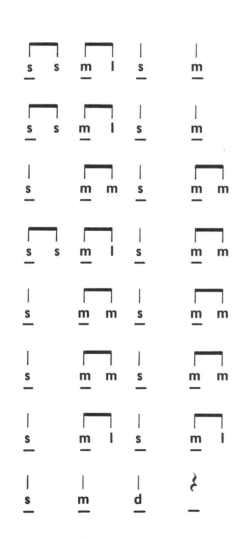

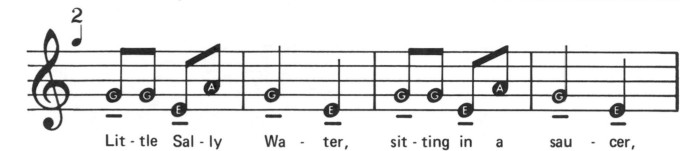

Lit - tle Sal - ly Wa - ter, sit - ting in a sau - cer,

Rise, Sal - ly, rise, Sal - ly, dry your weep-ing eyes, Sal - ly.

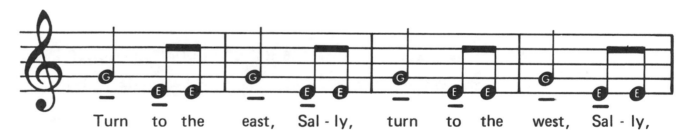

Turn to the east, Sal - ly, turn to the west, Sal - ly,

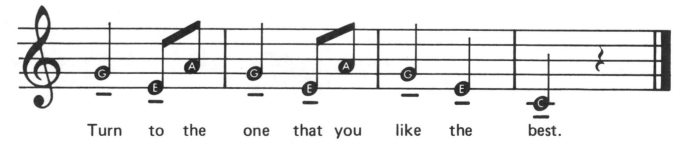

Turn to the one that you like the best.

Activity: Circle game. Do actions to words.
May use paper plate for Sally's saucer.
Chosen child is next "Sally."
Some prefer to do this with Sally's eyes closed on last two lines.

Using Rhythm In Stories

Hiawatha (may use finger puppets to illustrate rhythm)

Once there was an Indian boy who lived long ago, and his name was:

He did not live in the same type of house that you and I live in. His house was called a

What was his name?    Where did he live?

Now, three teepees down the left on Geronimo Avenue lived his girl friend. He walked

to   school   with   her   everyday   and   carried   her   books.   Her   name   was:

What was her name? (answer)   What was his name? (answer)

Now, when the two would meet, she would always say:  But after

they had been going together for a while, they were such good friends she just said:

More Rhythm In Stories

"Jack and the Beanstalk"—similar procedure

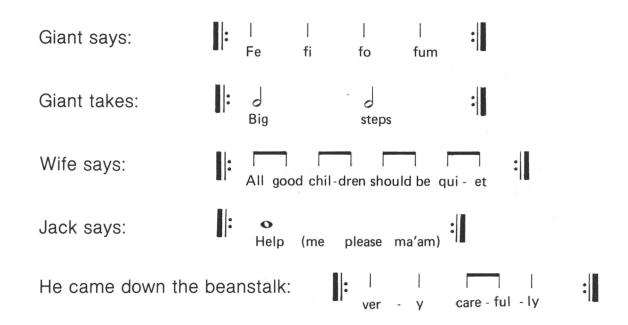

Giant says: ‖: | | | | :‖
Fe   fi   fo   fum

Giant takes: ‖: ♩   ♩ :‖
Big   steps

Wife says: ‖: ⌐⌐ ⌐⌐ ⌐⌐ ⌐⌐ :‖
All good chil-dren should be qui - et

Jack says: ‖: o :‖
Help (me   please   ma'am)

He came down the beanstalk: ‖: | | ⌐⌐ | :‖
ver - y   care - ful - ly

Extension: Four groups—each chants a sound with body percussion.

Snap—(Hiawatha/Fe, fi, fo, fum) ‖: | | | | :‖   **Later:** chant on *Sol* or G

Clap—(teepee/big steps) ‖: ♩   ♩ :‖   **Later:** chant on *Mi* or E

Patschen—(pretty Little Minnehaha/all good children should be quiet)

‖: ⌐⌐ ⌐⌐ ⌐⌐ ⌐⌐ :‖   **Later:** chant on *La* or A

Stamp—(How/Help) ‖: o :‖   **Later:** chant on *Do* or C

Mother, Mother I Am Sick

Tones Used:

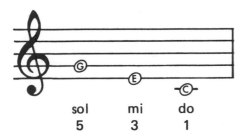

sol   mi   do
5   3   1

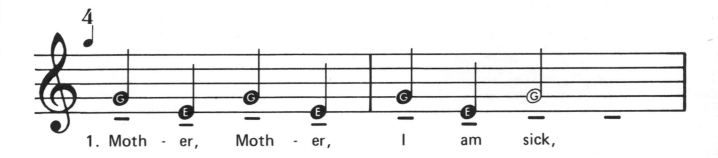

1. Moth - er,   Moth - er,   I   am   sick,

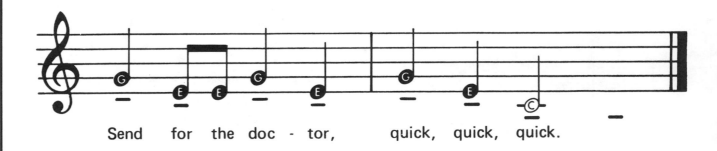

Send   for   the   doc - tor,   quick, quick, quick.

Emphasis:

- physical feeling of *Do*

- feeling of half-note ♩ (ta-a)

- use of arm signals

2. Send for the doctor, send for the nurse,

   send for the lady with the alligator purse

3. In came the doctor, *etc.* . . . .

4. Don't want the doctor, *etc.* . . . .

5. Out went the doctor, *etc.* . . . . .

Formation: (Circle if desired)

Kneel on floor, sit back on heels. Touch palms together, hands held high for *Sol*. Bring hands to knees for *Mi*. Lean over and touch floor with two fists, head down, for *Do* ("Praise Allah" position). Sing while doing this.

Fun to dramatize:

the patient, mother, messenger, doctor, nurse, and lady.

The Sun Is Shining And I Feel So Good

Canon

A beginning rhythm canon with speech and movement (Orff demonstration)

(A canon is a *round* that does not repeat over and over.)

The sun is shining and I feel so good. _

A. **Echo**
  1. T. begins chant, taps top of own head with both hands,
     on steady beat.
  2. Ch. *echo* chant *and* motion.
  3. T. repeats chant—claps hands on beat.
  4. Ch. *echo.*
  5. Continue on levels: knees, turn in place, stoop down and tap on floor.

B. **Canon**
  Do as above, but do not wait for children to echo movement.
  Go immediately to next motion—i.e. while you tap your head, they watch.
  While you clap your hands, they tap their head. While you tap your knees, they
  clap their hands (all chanting), etc.

C. **Canon**
  Repeat B, only going from bottom up.

Extension:
Use other chants in similar ways, as: Al - i   Ba - ba   and the   For - ty   Thieves

Vary the motions.

On A Log

Tones Used:

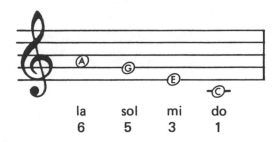

la	sol	mi	do
6	5	3	1

Emphasis:

- "Solami" phrase (Sol-La-Mi)

- arm signals as motions:

  Sol—palms together
  La—hands on shoulders
  Mi—palms on lap
  Do—fists tap sides of chair

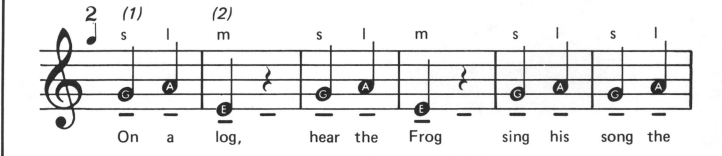

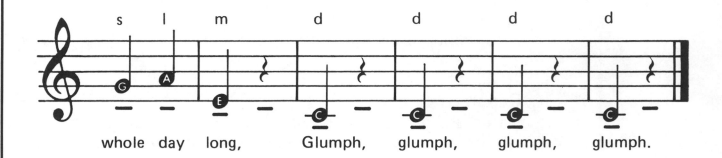

Although this may be sung as a lovely canon (in two groups, with group 2 beginning the song a measure after group 1), it should not be attempted with young children.

It may be sung when they are very secure with the teacher entering at the second measure. Later, a few may join her.

Five-Tone Songs* and Related Activities

**These songs also have the tone "Fa."

This section is for the preparation of the syllable

Re

The hand signal resembles
a "slippery slide."*

The arm signal is given by
raising the fingers of the palm
upward from the *Mi* position on the
knees.

Again: These are not to be named for the children in this preparation stage,
and are to be used only as body motions.

*Grace Nash

Hot Cross Buns

Tones Used:

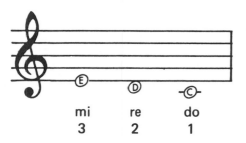

Emphasis:
- steady beat
- preparation for rest (⅟)
- dramatization

Extension:
This is usually the first tune a child learns to play by rote on the piano. The "set" of 3 black keys are used. Follow the numbers.

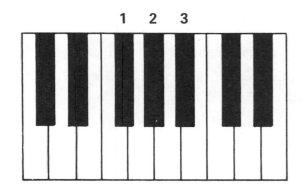

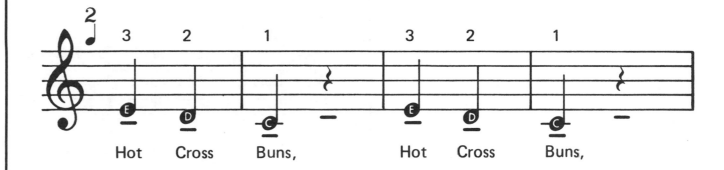

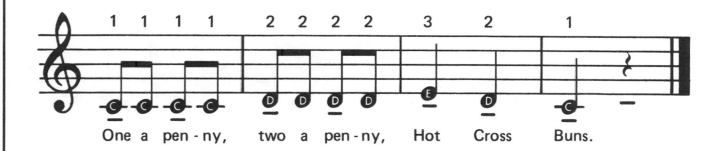

T. tell children how buns with a cross on the top made of icing are traditionally served for breakfast on Easter morning in several European countries.

They will enjoy the process of mixing ingredients, rolling the dough, cutting out, baking and decorating the buns (all in pantomime)—doing the motions to the steady beat while singing.

Hickety-Pickety Honey Cup

Tones Used:

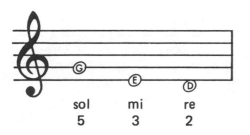

sol mi re
5 3 2

Emphasis:

- steady beat

NOTE: ♪ 6 meter moves in two's, so should pose no problem. Beats are underlined.

NOTE: The tonality of this song indicates the syllables *Do, La, Sol,* but may be used as *Sol, Mi, Re.*

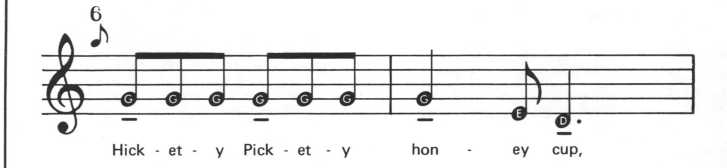

Hick - et - y Pick - et - y hon - ey cup,

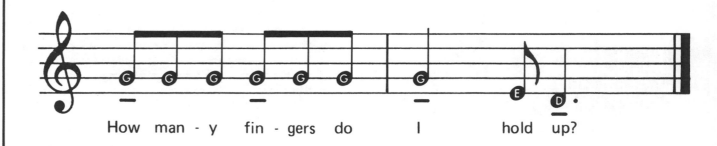

How man - y fin - gers do I hold up?

Spoken: *One* you said, and *three* there were
or: *Two* you said, and *Two* there were, and *so* you get another turn.

Activity: T. holds child across lap (spanking position) and bounces with knees while singing. She holds up any number of fingers between 1 and 5, child tries to guess. If correct, he gets a second turn.

Closet Key

Tones Used:

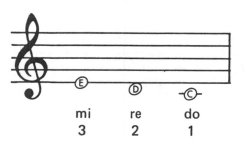

mi re do
3   2   1

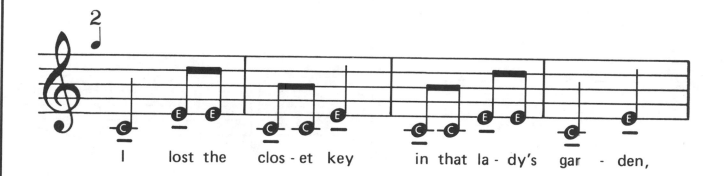

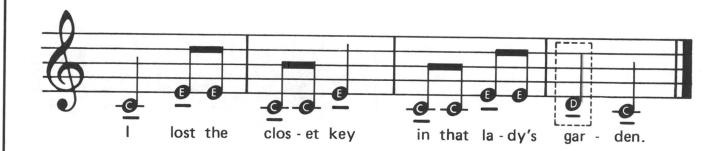

I lost the clos-et key in that la-dy's gar - den,

I lost the clos-et key in that la-dy's gar - den.

Emphasis:

- preparation for sound of *Re*
- individual singing:
  when song and game are well-known, the 3 persons can sing their parts individually.

E	mi
D	re
C	do

Extension:

Play the melody on the 3 bells, so the children can see. Ask "Who noticed something when I played the song?" *(Used middle bell only once.)* NOTE: Play only on the "bones" (beats) for this.

Game: Circle formation, hands cupped behind. One child, eyes closed, in center. Another child walks around outside during Verse I, and puts key in someone's hands.

Verse II—"Can't find the closet key . . . ." Child in center walks around and tries to guess who has it.

Verse III—"I found the closet key . . . ." Child who has key holds it up.

May rotate players: Key child to center, center child hides key, and outside child rejoins circle. Or each may choose a "good singer" to take their place.

Go To Sleep (Duerme Pronto)

Spanish folk song

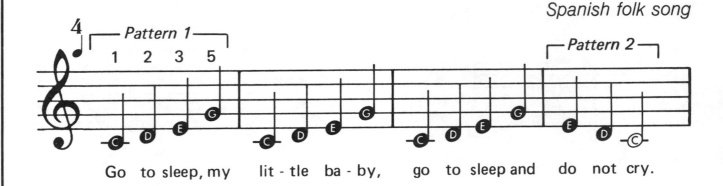

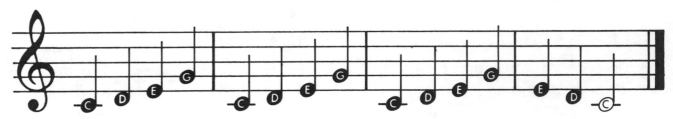

Go to sleep, my lit - tle ba - by, go to sleep and do not cry.

Moth - er's arms will hold you gent - ly, while she sings a lul - la - by.

Tones Used:

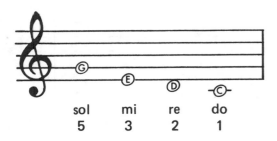

sol   mi   re   do
5   3   2   1

Emphasis:

- Experimental playing on the bells.

  Let the children watch as the melody is played on the bells. Help them discover there are only 2 patterns: 1-2-3-5 and 3-2-1

T. plays first pattern, a child plays second—then reverse.

Let two children do this.

Let several try complete song. THEY MUST SING!

Spanish Words:

Duerme pronto, niño mia, duerme pronto sin llorar,
que_estás en los brazos de tu madre que te va_a cantar.

T. "Who has a baby at your house. If the baby is crying, what could you do to help it go to sleep?"

Ch. Demonstrate ways of rocking, walking, patting the baby.
Teach song—repeat *slower* and *softer* (concepts reinforced).
Lay the baby down. Sh-h-h-h.

Frog In The Meadow

Tones Used:

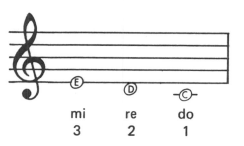

mi   re   do
3   2   1

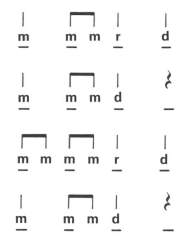

Traditional

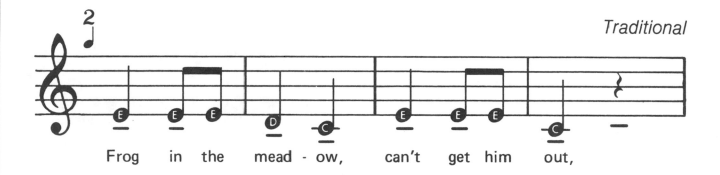

Frog   in   the   mead - ow,   can't   get   him   out,

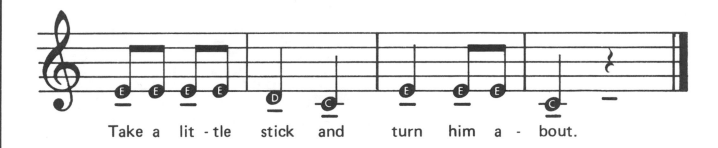

Take a   lit -tle   stick   and   turn   him a - bout.

Spoken:

Leap,   leap,   leap,   down.

Emphasis:

- *Mi, Re, Do* in a descending pattern
- Spoken part

Game: *Leap frog* Four children (frogs) squatting down one behind the other, hands tucked under body. Fifth child stands behind last one with a stick to ''stir'' end frog. On words ''Leap,'' the fourth child leaps over the others, and goes down in front on the word ''Down.'' Song repeats until all have gone through. The frogs then hop over and choose some ''good singers'' to take their place; continue.

Five Little Squirrels*

Finger Play

Speech with Instruments

Instruments:

Five little squirrels sat in a tree. _

First—Bass Xylophone (or)
Wood Block

(First instrument player speaks and plays on underlined words.)
The first one said: "What do you see?" _

Second—Alto Xylophone (or)
Rhythm Sticks

(Second instrument player)
The second one said: "A man with a gun." _

Third—Alto Glockenspiel (or)
Triangle

(Third instrument player)
The third one said: "We'd better run." _

Fourth—Metallaphone (or)
Maracas

(Fourth instrument player)
The fourth one said: "Let's hide in the shade." _

Fifth—Soprano Glock (or)
Tambourine

(Fifth instrument player)
The fifth one said: "I'm not afraid," When

(All instruments)

Gun—Drum

BANG *(drum)* went the gun. Away they did run. _

*Activity—Annie Mary Jones

Hop Old Squirrel

Tones Used:

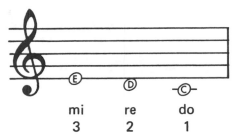

mi re do
3   2   1

Emphasis:

- Preparation for *Re*

- GAME: (circle, or scattered) Three hops forward, patschen on sound of words "eidle-dum, eidle-dum." Three hops back, patschen on eidle-dum.

Variety:

"Walk, old squirrel"
"Fly old squirrel"
"Sniff, old squirrel"

What else can the squirrel do?

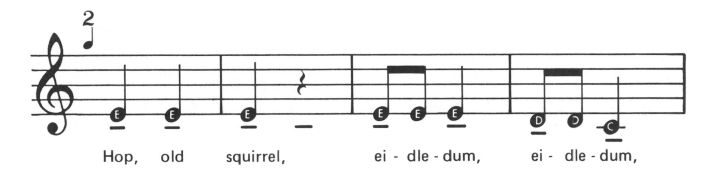

Hop, old squirrel, ei - dle - dum, ei - dle - dum,

Hop, old squirrel, ei - dle - dum dee.

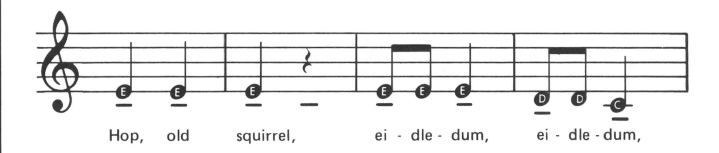

Hop, old squirrel, ei - dle - dum, ei - dle - dum,

Hop, old squirrel, ei - dle - dum dee.

Let Us Chase The Squirrel

Tones Used:

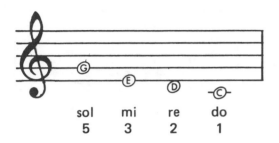

sol	mi	re	do
5	3	2	1

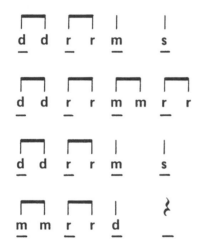

Let us chase the squir - rel, up the hick-'ry, down the hick-'ry,

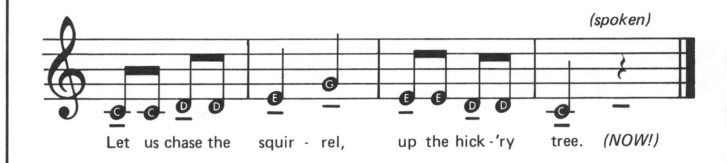

(spoken)

Let us chase the squir - rel, up the hick-'ry tree. *(NOW!)*

Game:

Version I—Children (trees) stand in a circle, hands cupped behind them. "It" (the "squirrel") walks on outside of circle during song, and drops small object (the "nut") in one child's hands.

At the end of the song, when all say "Now!", the child with the nut chases the squirrel around the circle to the opening (the "nest"). The new child is now the squirrel. Repeat with song.

Version II

Children are seated on floor in a circle, with space between. The squirrel walks in and out on the beat. On word "Now!" the person he is closest to gets up and follows him. Continue until all are up. Last one will be new squirrel.

All Around The Buttercup

Denise Bacon
used with permission

Tones Used:

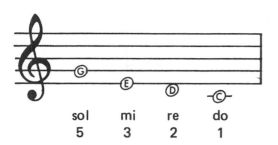

sol mi re do
 5   3   2   1

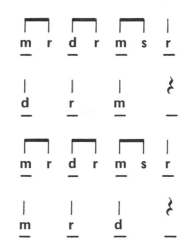

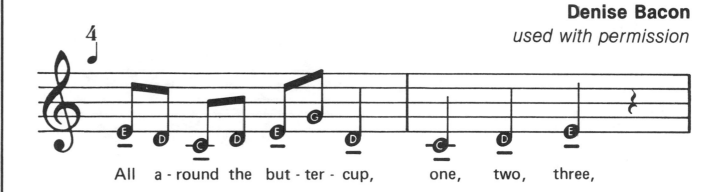

All a-round the but-ter-cup,   one,   two,   three,

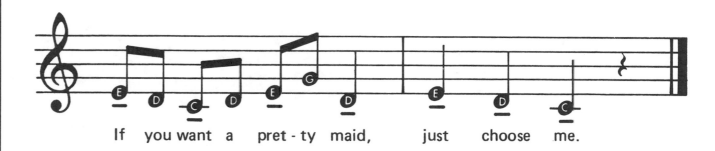

If you want a pret-ty maid,   just   choose   me.

Emphasis:
- steady beat
- slower tempo
- feeling for rest (𝄼)

Extension: *Halloween* All around the witch's tree, 1, 2, 3. If you want a mean old witch, just choose me.

Circle Game

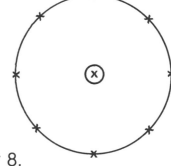

Note: It is better to use small groups—preferably 6 or 8.

Outside children hold hands and walk slowly in a circle, stepping the steady beat. On words "just choose me", the child in the middle points to one in the circle. That one remains in place, but turns to outside, rejoining hands. Continue until all are circling with their backs to center. At the end, all "wilt," and sink to floor.

Bow-Wow-Wow

Tones Used:

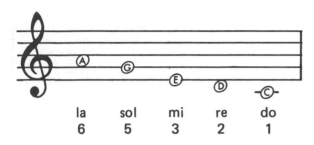

la sol mi re do
6   5   3 2   1

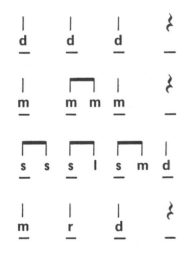

Emphasis:
- game
- preparation for *Re*

Note: Excellent as song and action round for older children. 2, 3, or 4 circles, all doing the game, but beginning one measure apart.

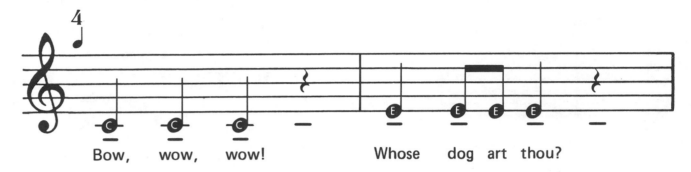

Bow, wow, wow!   Whose dog art thou?

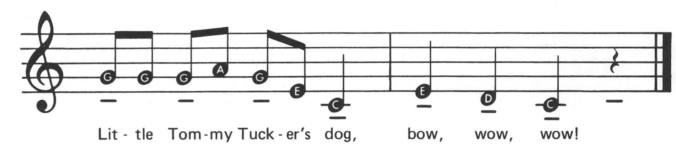

Lit-tle Tom-my Tuck-er's dog, bow, wow, wow!

Game: Single circle, partners facing. "Bow, wow, wow"—stamp L, R, L. "Whose dog . . ."—with a jerk point R. finger up about nose high (clapping first). "Little . . ."—partners hold both hands, circle just to change places (not a complete circle). "Bow, . . ."—jump 3 times, turning back on partner; now face new partner, begin again.

Note: With young ones beginning—suggest all sit in circle, begin with just 2, and add on a new set of partners each time.

Extension: T. clap: | | | ⸪ Ask, "What words did I clap?" Continue by phrases. Ask: "Who can clap the words that come next?" Continue until they can clap the whole song through. This comes later, after many days of singing and playing the game.

Here Comes A Bluebird

Tones Used:

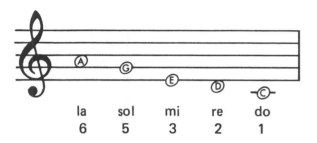

la	sol	mi	re	do
6	5	3	2	1

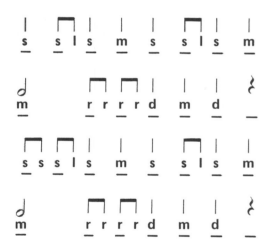

Emphasis:

- feeling of question/answer in music
- feeling of 𝅗𝅥 (ta-a)
- game

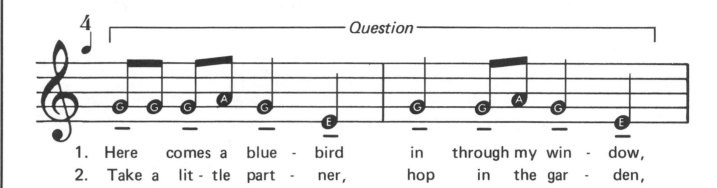

1. Here comes a blue - bird in through my win - dow,
2. Take a lit - tle part - ner, hop in the gar - den,

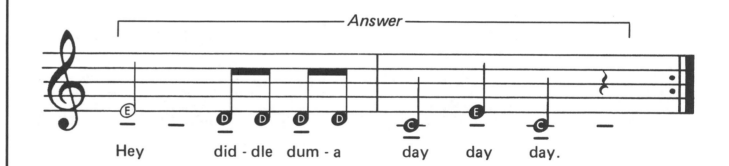

Hey did - dle dum - a day day day.

Provide background—picture or story. "How does a bird move?" Fly—hop.

T. sings song, asks "How could bird come through a window?" Ch. discuss.

Were there "funny" words in song? Did they mean anything?

T. sings again, then sings first phrase, ch. echo. Continue.

T. "If I sing the first part, can you sing the part that comes next?" Continue.

Game: Circle formation, hold hands up for windows. One child, the bluebird, goes in and out on first part, chooses a partner and "hops in the garden" with him on second part. Repeat, with new person as next bluebird. Or—may be accumulative with 2, then 4, etc. There are many variants of this song.

Developing Inner Hearing

Children have a vital need to internalize sound.

The "Radio Game" may be used to develop this:

    (Discuss what happens to the sound when the radio is turned off.)

T. turns song or rhyme "off and on" while the children are singing or chanting.

This should be done at natural-feeling phrases, and not too rapidly.

It may be advisable to precede this with turning the volume "knob" *softer*, then *louder* on alternating phrases before doing *off* and *on*.

Example: (click-on!) "Hickory, Dickory, Dock, the mouse ran up the clock,

(turn knob to make it *softer*) The clock struck one, the mouse ran down,

(turn volume to make it *louder*) Hickory, Dickory, Dock." (Click off!)

Face Puppets For Inner Hearing

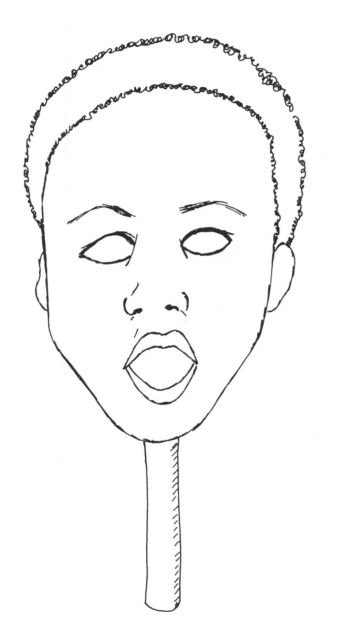

Face puppets may
be used for the same
effect as the Radio Game.
These should be made about the same size as a child's face.
They may be glued back to back on a stick or ruler for easier turning. Turn for sound
and silence phrases.

Hey, Mr. Monday

Tones Used:

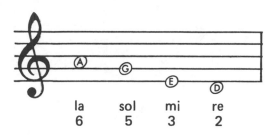

la sol mi re
6   5   3   2

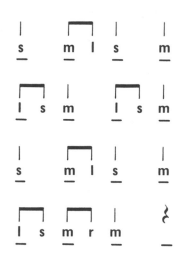

(Adapted)

Barbara Andress

used with permission *

Hey,   Mis - ter   Mon - day,   sing a song,   sing a song,

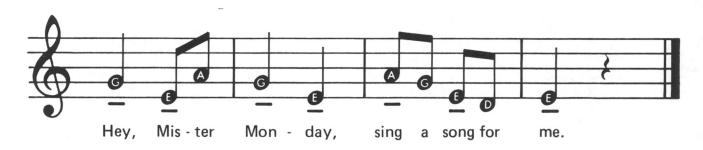

Hey,   Mis - ter   Mon - day,   sing a song for   me.

Procedure: Form a circle, all walk in same direction while singing each time. On interludes, stop in place.

1. Sing and walk beat.
2. Stop and clap the words.
3. Sing and walk beat.
4. Stop and think the words.
5. Sing and walk beat.

(May stop here depending on age and experience of children.)

6. Stop and clap something else in that space.

7. Sing and walk beat.
8. Do something else with instruments in that space

(Find someone that understands— others watch Susie.)

May go through days of the week.

* *from Exploring Music TE2*
© 1975 Holt Rinehart & Winston

Emphasis:

- steady beat
- inner hearing
- beginning improvisation

Cobbler, Cobbler, Mend My Shoe

Tones Used:

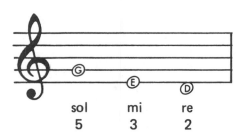

sol   mi   re
5   3   2

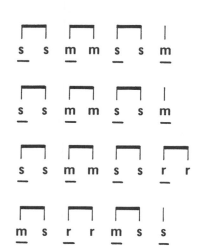

s s m m s s m

s s m m s s m

s s m m s s r r

m s r r m s s

Emphasis:

- steady beat
- preparation for syllable *Re*

Note: Bell numbers are used to aid in T. preparation of interval *Sol-Re*

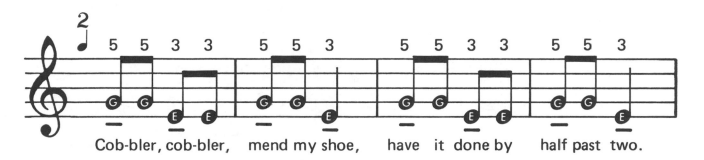

Cob-bler, cob-bler,   mend my shoe,   have it done by   half past two.

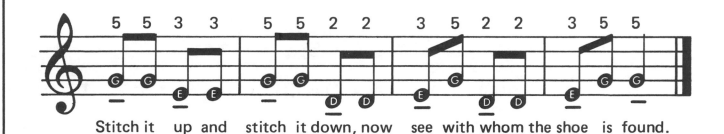

Stitch it   up and   stitch it down, now   see with whom the shoe   is found.

Game: Children sit in a circle, hands behind them. One child in the center is the *cobbler.* He hides his eyes during song while others pass a shoe from one to another. (See that the shoe is passed continuously—it tends to "bog" down.) At the end of the song, the person who has it holds it behind his back while cobbler tries to guess who has the shoe. After 3 guesses, he trades places with the person who had the shoe; the game continues.

Variation: Cross leg; double fist, "hammer on" shoe sole to feel steady beat.

Demonstration number **Wee Willie Winkie** **and** ⟶

Suggested Procedure:

1. Eight beats (for clock sounds). Use gong or cymbal, then

2. Begin ostinato pattern: | | | ≀ for eight beats, then continue during poem.
pat pat pat snap

3. All children recite in a soft voice:

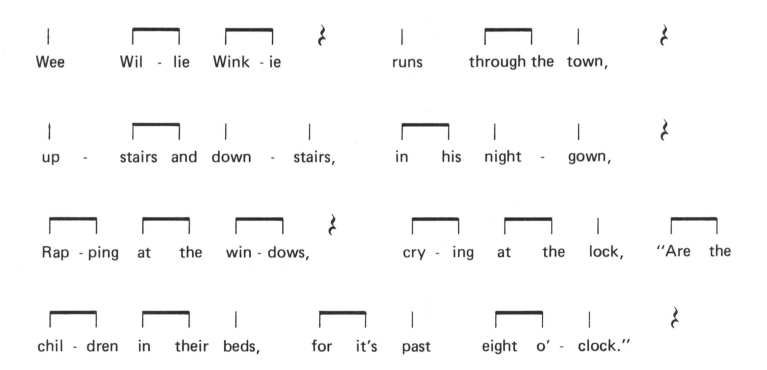

Wee   Wil - lie   Wink - ie   runs   through the town,

up -   stairs and down - stairs,   in   his   night - gown,

Rap - ping   at   the   win - dows,   cry - ing   at   the   lock,   "Are   the

chil - dren   in   their beds,   for   it's   past   eight o' - clock."

4. All stretch and give a big yawn   H-o   Hu-m

Noddin'

Tones Used:

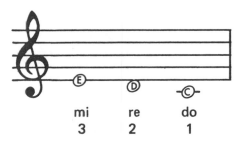

mi   re   do
3   2   1

Emphasis:

- dramatize
- ostinato
- half notes ♩ (ta-a)

Note: song begins on an
"up-beat" or "pick-up"

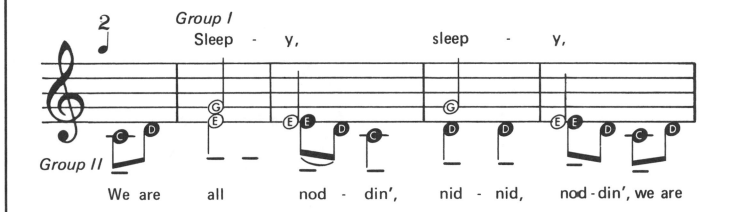

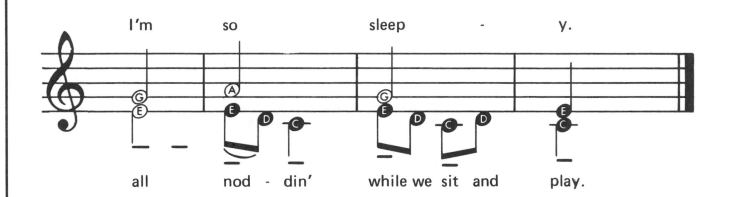

5. Group I sings their part through one time alone.
   (Use just about ¼ of your class for this group.)

6. Group I sings a second time *with* Group II singing the melody.
   (Do this twice.) Don't forget to nod!

7. All heads still, all eyes closed—one child gives a loud snore and whistle.

Lines and Spaces

Point of Confusion: In classroom letter writing, we tell the children to write

their letters *on the line:*

Then, in music, we tell them to write their *notes on the line:*

Here are two aids to help the distinction:

The Ladder	**Simon Says**

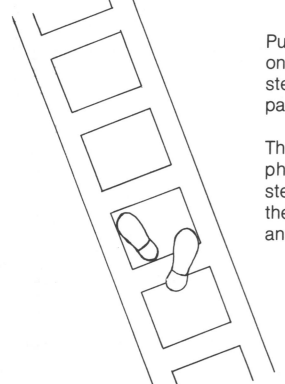

Put a masking-tape ladder on the floor. Use only 5 steps, as this is also preparation for staff notation.

The children will get the physical experience of stepping *on* the lines, and *in* the spaces, also going *up* and *down*

Have the children use their heads for "notes."

Simon says: 'Make a space note."

Simon says: "Make a line note."

"Make a space note!"
Ah-ha! Caught-cha!

See The Little Ducklings

Tones Used:

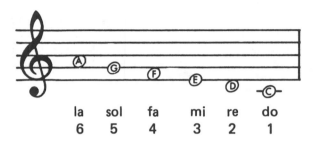

la	sol	fa	mi	re	do
6	5	4	3	2	1

Emphasis:

- phrasing (musical sentences)

- melody line
  (a melody can go only 3 ways: up, down, or stay the same)

- rest
  When singing the song, flap your wings at the end of each phrase.

Note:

The syllable *Fa* is used here. It is *F* or *4* on your bells.

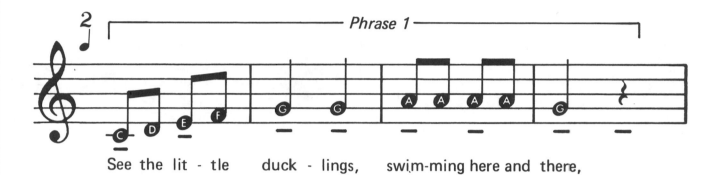

See the lit - tle duck - lings, swim-ming here and there,

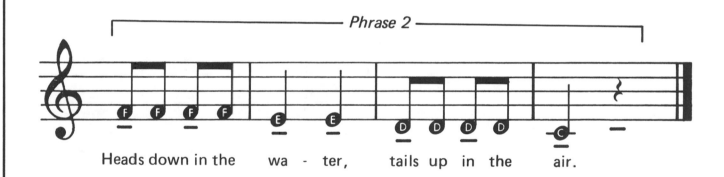

Heads down in the wa - ter, tails up in the air.

Phrase 1: Make a large arc with one arm, while thumb and fingers "quack" on steady beat.

Phrase 2: Make a large arc again, while duck's head (thumb and fingers) bobs down in the water on steady beat.

Use the little felt ducklings in your math kit—arrange them on the felt board to show the notes going up, staying the same, and coming down.

Twinkle, Twinkle, Little Star

Tones Used:

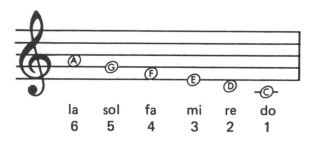

la · sol · fa · mi · re · do
6 · 5 · 4 · 3 · 2 · 1

Emphasis:

Movement for
- feeling of phrases (a musical sentence)

- feeling of the form ABA (three parts: first and last are the same, the middle is different.)

- half-note ♩ (ta-a)

Note: The tone "F" is used here as the *Fa* syllable.

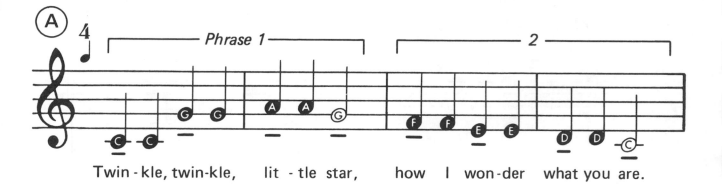

Twin-kle, twin-kle,   lit-tle star,   how I won-der what you are.

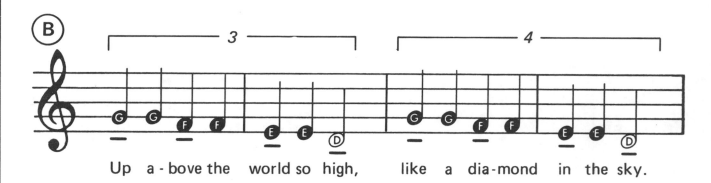

Up a-bove the   world so high,   like a dia-mond in the sky.

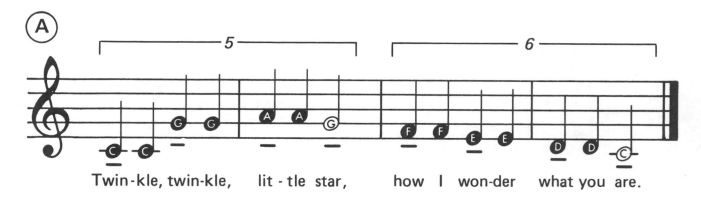

Twin-kle, twin-kle,   lit-tle star,   how I won-der what you are.

In this song, the *steps* are *underlined* for the movement, and *not* the *steady beats.*

Movement for "Twinkle, Twinkle, Little Star"

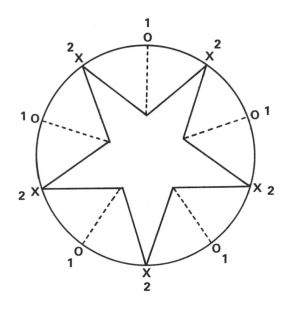

Ten children stand in a circle—either boy-girl, or count off one's and two's.

Note: It helps children to remember their number if they are touched on one shoulder for "one," and both shoulders for "two."

The children hold either a stretch rope, or a circle made of about 6 yards of elastic. The places to hold their hands should be marked or taped. They should hold the elastic with both hands close together in front of the waist.

A—the "one's" step in on phrase *one. Count:* "step, step, step, hold."
Phrase *two, count:* "Back, back, back, hold."

B—on phrase *three*, all lift arms slowly. *Count:* "Up, up, up, hold."
Phrase *four*, lower arms. "Down, down, down, hold."

A—the "two's" repeat what the "one's" did on phrases *five* and *six*.

Tones Used:

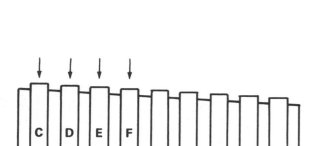

fa   mi   re   do
4   3   2   1

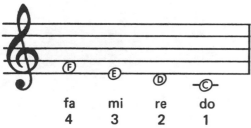

Juba (Version 1)

"Juba" has been done as a dance, song, hand-clap, or play, in several ways.

"Juba" evidently refers to giblets, and other mixed together foods.

This version is partly sung, and partly chanted to much clapping.

Traditional

Ju - ba this and   Ju - ba that,   Ju - ba killed a   yel - low cat.

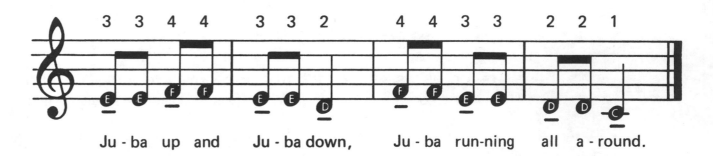

Ju - ba up and   Ju - ba down,   Ju - ba run-ning   all a - round.

Juba (Version 2*)

Tones Used:

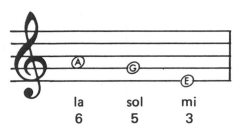

la sol mi
6 5 3

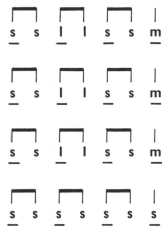

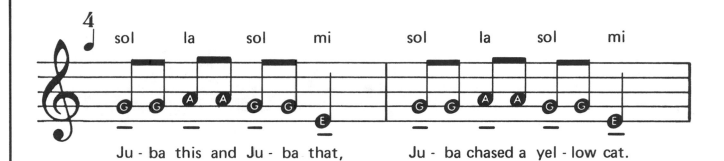

sol la sol mi | sol la sol mi

Ju - ba this and Ju - ba that, | Ju - ba chased a yel - low cat.

sol la sol mi | sol sol sol sol

Ju - ba up and Ju - ba down, | Ju - ba turn-ing all a - round.

Game: (*Involving arm signals*) Use on beats only (underlined), not on rhythm. Partner game—clap own hands for *Sol*, partner's hand for *La*, own thighs for *Mi*. Final phrase, turn in place (4 steps) while clapping hands for *Sol*.

Note: Begin with just T. and one child. They each then choose someone else and ''teach'' them; those 4 each choose another, etc.

Emphasis:

• arm signals in a game activity

*Aden Lewis workshop

Part VI

Songs In Other Keys

Home Plate Moves

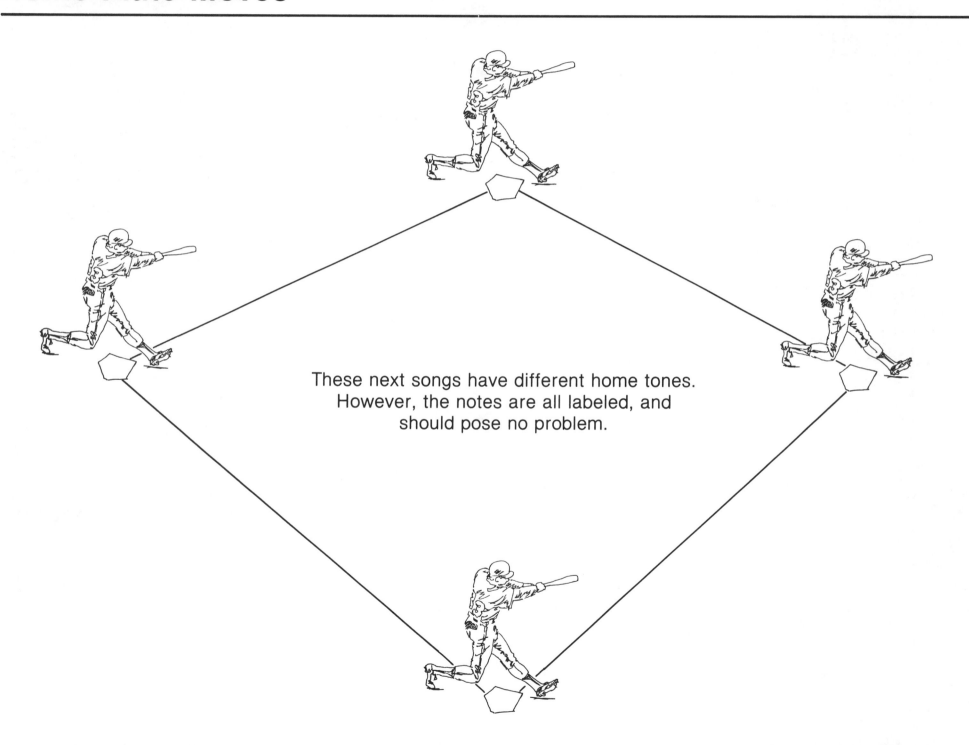

These next songs have different home tones.
However, the notes are all labeled, and
should pose no problem.

Down Came A Lady

(This song has a different home tone.)

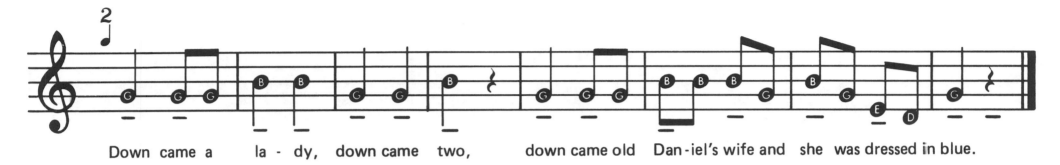

Down came a la - dy, down came two, down came old Dan-iel's wife and she was dressed in blue.

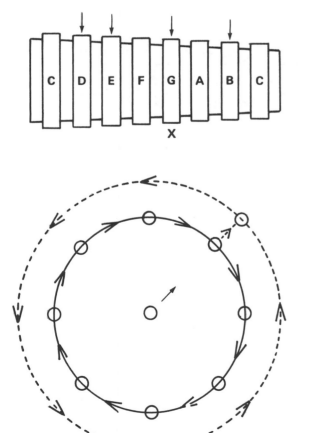

Game: *Circle formation.* Do not hold hands. One child is in the middle. All children sing the song and walk the beat in one direction.

On the last word, *blue*, the child in the center points to someone and says a color they have on. (Or, they may just continue to say "*blue.*") That person immediately drops out of the circle and begins walking in the opposite direction.

Try to keep the song going and not stop each time.

Continue until all in the first circle are now in outer circle. At the last, all stop and point to the middle child and say his color.

("Clap the beat, and sing as you go back to your chairs.")

Ten In The Bed

Finger-Play/Game

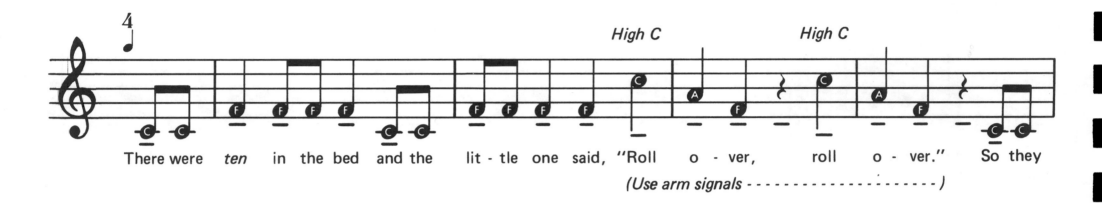

There were *ten* in the bed and the lit - tle one said, "Roll o - ver, roll o - ver." So they

(Use arm signals -)

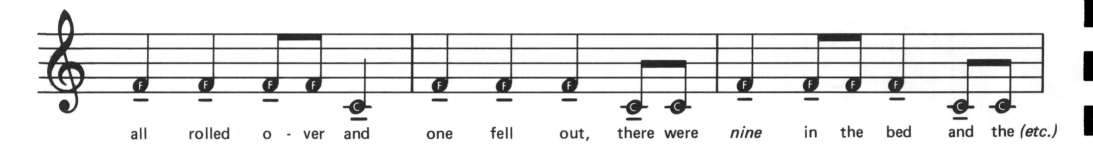

all rolled o - ver and one fell out, there were *nine* in the bed and the *(etc.)*

Continue until: There was *one* in the bed, and the little one said,

"I've got the whole bed to myself!*"

Add Claps! Swings! Movement! Line up 10 chairs, let the children "roll over" and fall on the floor on their number.

*from Pat Hensley

Go Tell Aunt Rhody

A Sing-To-Me Song

(This song has a different home tone.)

Set the mood of the song by telling the "story" of the mill pond.

Children call: "Aunt Rhody! Aunt Rhody!" (unpitched, but with voice inflection)

Traditional

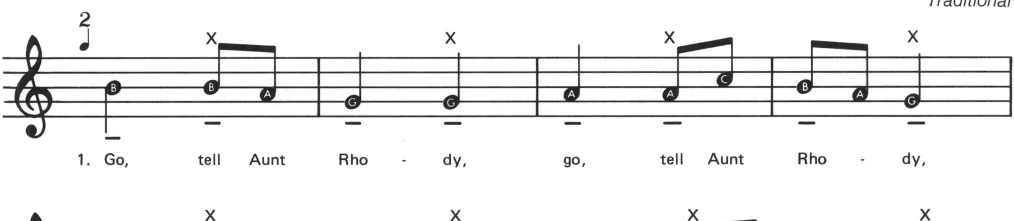

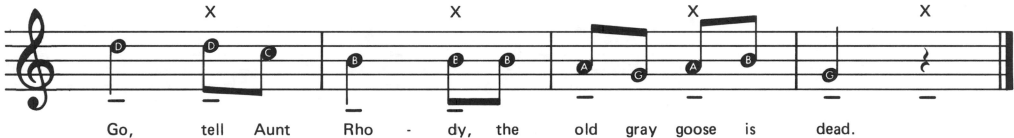

x—lightly play finger cymbals, triangle, or high D on bells.

2. She died in the mill pond . . . standing on her head.

3. The goslings are crying . . . the old gray goose is dead.

4. The gander is weeping . . . the old gray goose is dead.

5. Repeat verse I.

A beautiful Orff arrangement may be found in *Music With Children,* Grace Nash, Series I

Five Little Ducks

A Sing-To-Me Song

Tones Used:

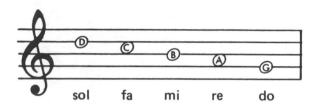

sol   fa   mi   re   do

Emphasis:

- sing to the children
- finger play
- dramatize

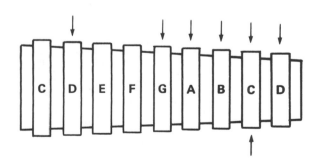

The "C" used here is the high C.

(This has a different home tone.)

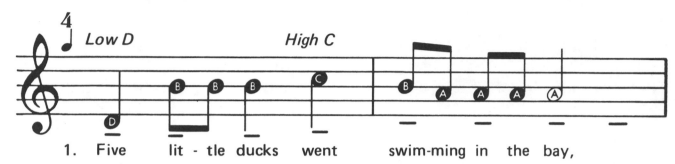

1. Five   lit - tle ducks went   swim-ming in   the   bay,

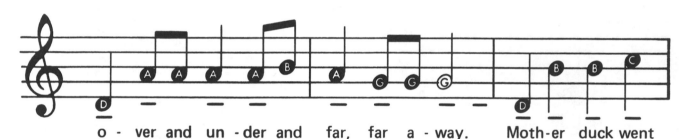

o - ver and un - der and   far, far a - way.   Moth-er duck went

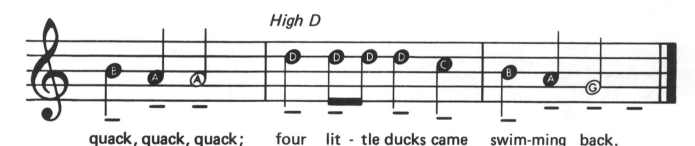

quack, quack, quack;   four   lit - tle ducks came   swim-ming   back.

2. Four little ducks . . . three little ducks . . . .
3. Three little ducks . . . two . . . .
4. Two little ducks . . . one . . . .
5. One little duck . . . no . . . .
6. No little ducks . . .
   Father Duck went Quack, Quack, Quack,
   Five little ducks, came swimming back.

Mary Wore Her Red Dress

Tones Used:

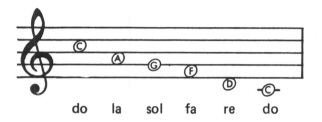

do la sol fa re do

Emphasis:

- individual singing
- discovering rhythm in their names.

Texas folk song

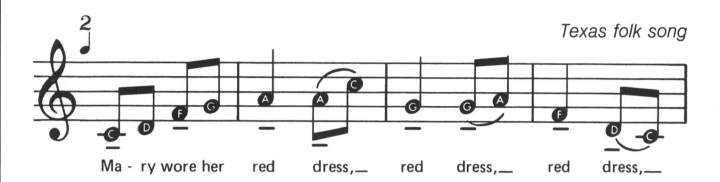

Ma - ry wore her red dress,— red dress,— red dress,—

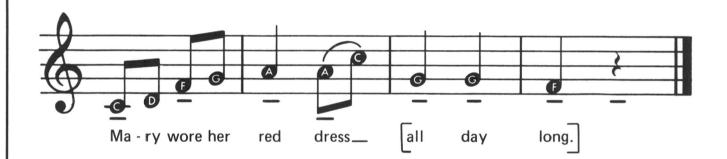

Ma - ry wore her red dress— [all day long.]

Suggestion:

T. sings all except "all day long;" let individual children sing that part.

Substitute other names:

- Arturo wore his blue jeans.

Show how their names look in a rhythm pattern:

Mary —— ——
Arturo — —— —
Brad ——

This And That For Special Days

*Songs

Happy Birthday!

Birthday Ring
Version I

Birthday Ring
Version II

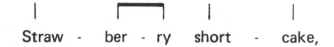

Straw - ber - ry short - cake,

Huck - le - ber - ry Finn,

When I call your birth - day month,

Jump in!

Jan - u - ar - y, Feb - ru - ar - y, *etc.*

| | | | |
1, 2, 3, 4,

| | | |
5, 6, 7, 8,

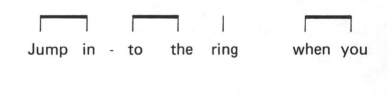

Jump in - to the ring when you

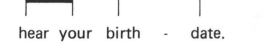

hear your birth - date.

Jan - u - ar - y, Feb - ru - ar - y, *etc.*

Repeat rhyme to jump
out of the ring.

Repeat to jump *out.*

The County Fair

(usually first week in October)

"The Parade"

Emphasis:

- steady beat (beats are underlined in chant)

- dynamics (loud and soft)

- ABA form
  (in enrichment song) ABA: 3 parts of music. The first and last are the same, the middle is different.

Discuss how the parade sounds when far down the street—how it sounds when closer, how it sounds as it goes by you, and on down the street.

(pick-up)

Chant: Hear the | beat, beat, beat of the | feet, feet, feet,

Of the | children as they march on the | street, street, street.

Activity:

1. Place index fingers flat on edge of desk. Alternate them to show steady beat while chant is said softly.
2. Repeat chant using 2 fingers each hand—voices slightly louder.
3. Repeat chant using 3 fingers each hand—voices slightly louder.
4. Repeat chant using 4 fingers each hand—voices louder.
5. Repeat chant, dropping back to 3 fingers each hand—voices slightly softer.
6. Repeat chant, dropping back to 2 fingers each hand—voices slightly softer.
7. Repeat chant, dropping back to 1 finger each hand—voices soft.

Enrichment: "Oh, Dear, What Can The Matter Be?"—old nursery song. Children love to link arms and sway during first and last part of song; for middle part, shake finger on steady beat.

Columbus Day

(October 12)

Columbus

Tune: "Farmer In The Dell"

1. Columbus was so brave,
   Columbus was so brave,
   Heigh - ho, the derry - oh
   Columbus was so brave.

2. He traveled far by sea . . . .

3. He said, "Sail on and on." . . . .

4. His ships they numbered three . . . .

5. The first was the Nina . . . .

6. The second was the Pinta . . . .

7. The third was the Santa Maria . . . .

8. We love our land today . . . etc.

Sailor's Chant*

(stamp)

heave   ho,   heave   ho

(patschen)

ship   a - hoy,   ship   a - hoy

(clap)

pull on the rope,   pull on the rope

(snap & pull)

pull,   pull

Expansion: "Can you lock up the words in your head and let your body sounds say them?"

Later: Let a few that are secure in their rhythm use rhythm instruments in place of body percussion.

*Myra Wharton—used with permission

Fireman, Fireman, Number 8 *Chant/Song*

Tones Used:

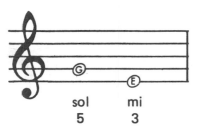

sol   mi
5   3

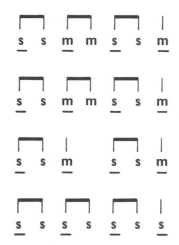

s s   m m   s s   m

s s   m m   s s   m

s s   m   s s   m

s s   s s   s s   s

Use as chant: Use hands levels "light" (high) "dark" (low) or "medium" (middle) voices. Let children take turns directing, breaking level in several places. Use "funny" voices for emphasis.

(Fire Prevention Week, usually second week in October.)

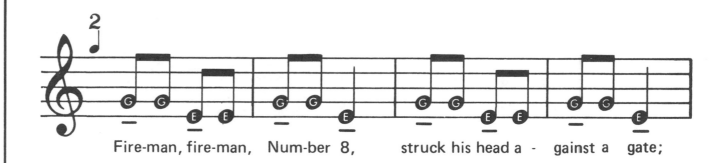

Fire-man, fire-man, Num-ber 8,   struck his head a - gainst a gate;

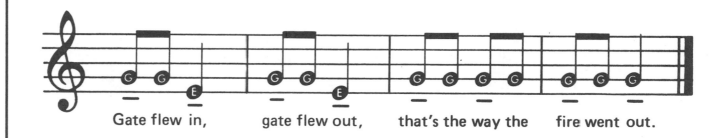

Gate flew in,   gate flew out,   that's the way the   fire went out.

Spoken: "squirt, squirt, swish, swish."

Activity: Two circles—partners face one another. Sing and use arm signals on *beat* as indicated on the left. Clap own hands for *Sol,* patschen for *Mi.* Turn in place four walking steps on last measure.

Then everyone takes one step close to the right on words, "squirt, squirt", brush hands twice on words "swish, swish." They will now be facing a new partner. Repeat and continue until back to first partner.

Which Witch?

adapted by Wilma Salzman

Counting-out rhyme: Touch each child on steady beat. Use "witchy" voice tones.

Or, actions may be pantomimed.

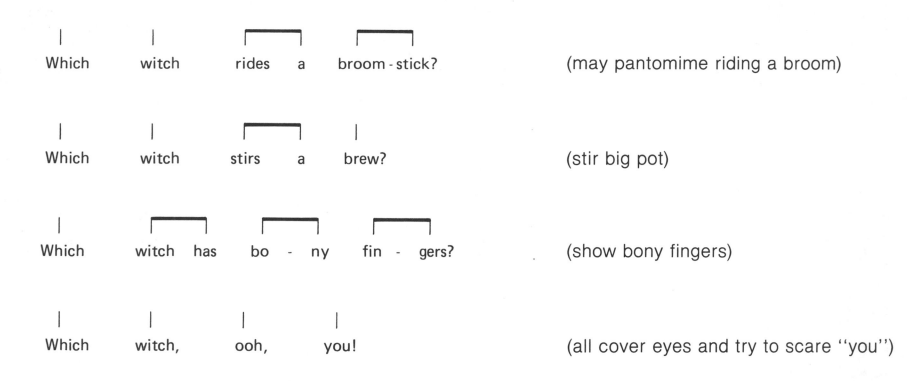

Which   witch   rides   a   broom - stick?   (may pantomime riding a broom)

Which   witch   stirs   a   brew?   (stir big pot)

Which   witch   has   bo - ny   fin - gers?   (show bony fingers)

Which   witch,   ooh,   you!   (all cover eyes and try to scare "you")

Note: Steady beats are underlined. Rhythm of each line is different.

Extension: When rhyme is well known, let children clap words as they recite the rhyme.

T. may clap the rhythm of one line. Ask: "What words did I clap?" Continue.

This can be a circle game with "it" (the witch) flying on a broom around the circle and scaring "you."

Old Mother Witch

Tones Used:

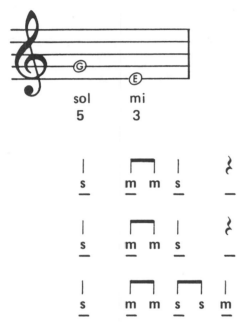

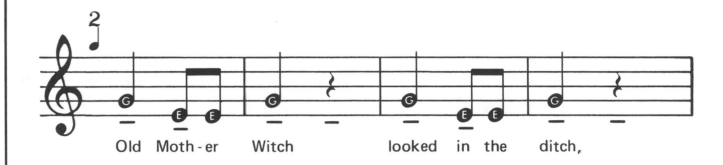

Old Moth-er Witch looked in the ditch,

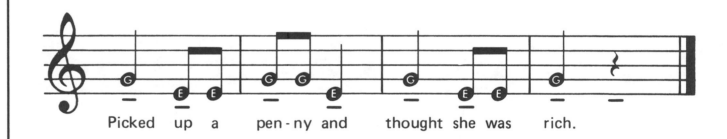

Picked up a pen-ny and thought she was rich.

More rhythm fun based on the natural rhythm phrase of a child:

- "Ghosts, ghosts, scary ghosts."
- "Witch, witch, mean old witch."
- "Bats, bats, flying bats." Let them expand on this.

T. (the witch) walks around room, 7 or 8 children following her. At the end of the song, she turns around and asks in a witchy voice. "Are you my children?" They all answer "No-o-o-o."

Repeat song and action—again they answer "No-o-o-o."

But—the third time, they answer "Yes!" and run back to their seats before the "witch" can catch them.

Ten Little Goblins

Traditional

Ten little goblins standing in a row.

(Hold fingers up straight.)

When they see the old witch they bow just so.

(Lower fingers on word 'bow', raise on 'so'.)

They march to the left and they march to the right

(Be sure to 'Mirror' this motion.)

Then they crawl in bed and they sleep all night.

(Double up fists, tuck under chin.)

Echo chant: T. use hand drum or tambourine to keep steady beat.

Five Old Turkeys

Tones Used:

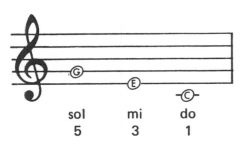

sol mi do
5 3 1

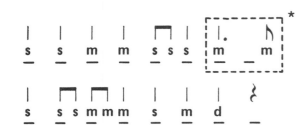

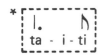
ta - i - ti

Emphasis:

- feeling of *Do*
- fingerplay
- dramatize, with children as turkeys.
- use stick puppets

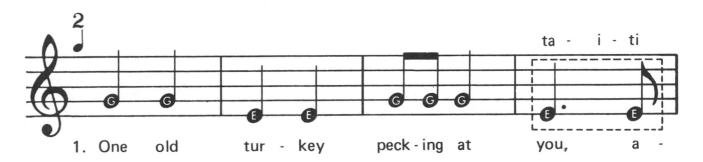

ta - i - ti

1. One old tur - key peck - ing at you, a -

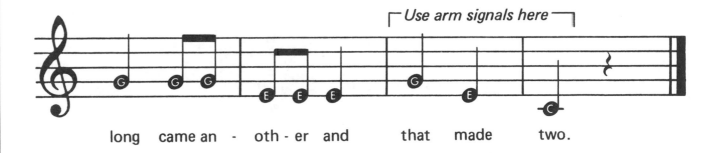

Use arm signals here

long came an - oth - er and that made two.

2. Two old turkeys flew up in a tree . . . three.

3. Three old turkeys flew around some more . . . four.

4. Four old turkeys walking down the drive . . . five.

5. Five old turkeys went behind a fence

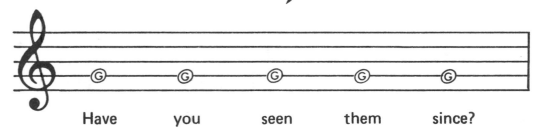

Have you seen them since?

Note: Sing song softly, as children are inclined to shout on number words.

Thanksgiving Fun

(Oldies But Goodies)

I. Tune: "Mulberry Bush"

(1) This is the way the Pilgrims walk, the Pilgrims walk, the Pilgrims walk,
This is the way the Pilgrims walk, Thanksgiving Day in the morning.

(Palms together in front—walk sedately.)

(2) This is the way the turkey struts . . . .

(Form wings, strut about the room.)

(3) This the way the Indians dance . . . .

II. Tune: "Lightly Row"

Pumpkin pie, pumpkin pie, come, my lady, come and buy.

Pumpkin pie, pumpkin pie, come and buy a pie.

Then your children will not cry, if they have a pumpkin pie.

Pumpkin pie, pumpkin pie, come and buy a pie.

Holiday Rhythm Chants

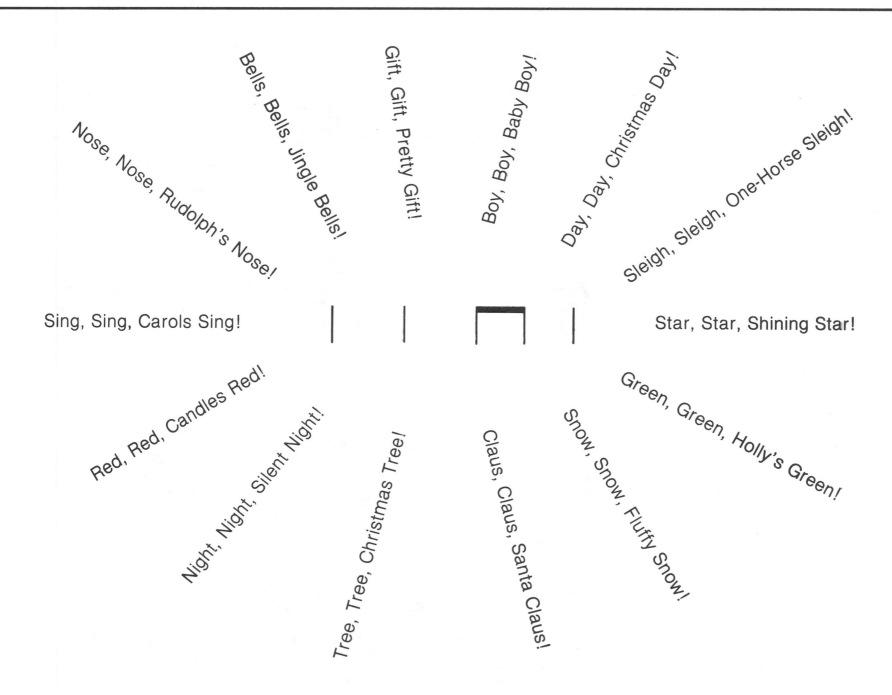

Bells, Bells, Jingle Bells!

Gift, Gift, Pretty Gift!

Boy, Boy, Baby Boy!

Day, Day, Christmas Day!

Nose, Nose, Rudolph's Nose!

Sleigh, Sleigh, One-Horse Sleigh!

Sing, Sing, Carols Sing!

Star, Star, Shining Star!

Red, Red, Candles Red!

Green, Green, Holly's Green!

Night, Night, Silent Night!

Snow, Snow, Fluffy Snow!

Tree, Tree, Christmas Tree!

Claus, Claus, Santa Claus!

Hanukkah

Jewish folk song

Tones Used:

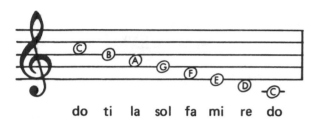

do ti la sol fa mi re do

Emphasis:

- help the children discover that the rhythm pattern of

  is the same on all four parts.

- add tambourines to play on the rhythm.

Note: It is easier for small children to play a tambourine if they hold it upside down in their lap and tap the rim with their hand.

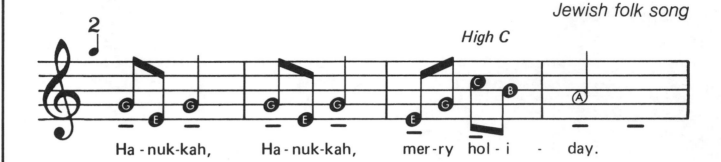

Ha - nuk-kah,   Ha - nuk-kah,   mer-ry hol-i - day.

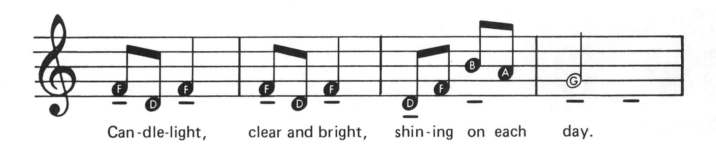

Can-dle-light,   clear and bright,   shin-ing on each   day.

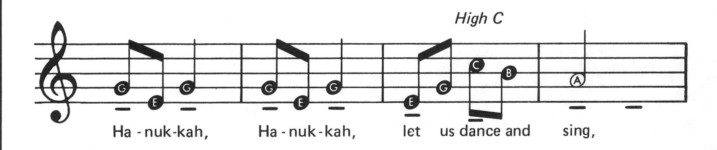

Ha - nuk-kah,   Ha - nuk-kah,   let us dance and   sing,

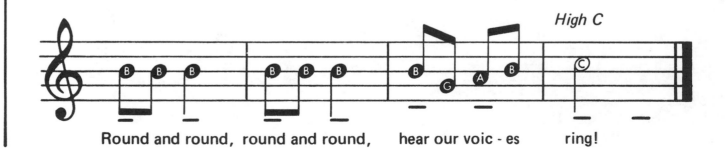

Round and round, round and round,   hear our voic - es   ring!

Mary Had A Baby

Spiritual

Tones Used:

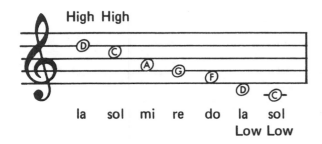

High High

D C
A
G
F
D C

la sol mi re do la sol
Low Low

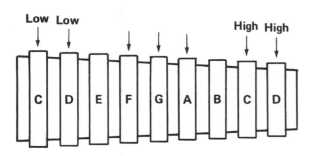

Low Low   High High

C D E F G A B C D

Effective Call and Response:

Group I: ''Mary had a baby''

Group II: ''Yes, Lord''

Together: ''The people keep a-comin' and the train's done gone.''

Note: Rhythm pattern: ta - i - ti

Ma - ry had a ba - by, yes, Lord,

Ma - ry had a ba - by, yes, my Lord.

High D *High C*

Ma - ry had a ba - by, yes, Lord, the

High C

peo - ple keep - a com - in' and the train's done gone.

2. Born in lowly stable . . .

3. Where did Mary lay Him . . .

4. Laid Him in a manger . . .

5. What did Mary name Him . . .

6. Mary named Him Jesus . . .

The New Year

Cecelia Jones
used with permission

Tones Used:

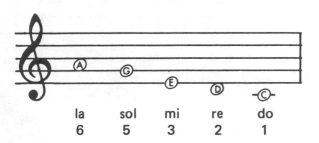

la	sol	mi	re	do
6	5	3	2	1

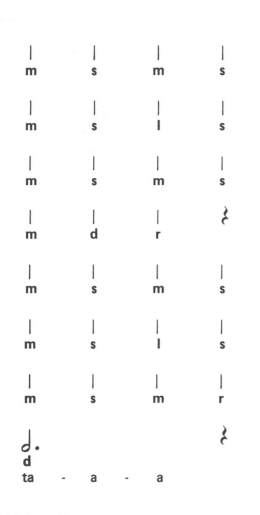

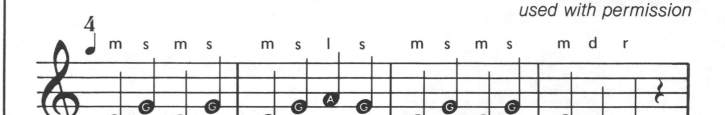

Jan - u - ar - y   is a new year, Feb - ru - ar - y   Val - en - tine,

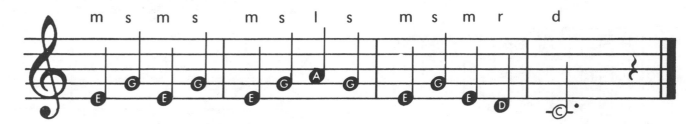

March - 's wind brings A - pril show - ers, May is flow - er   time.

*three beats —
count *ta-a-a*.

Emphasis

- sound of the interval *Mi-Sol*
- reinforcement of *Re*
- fun with arm signals (do not name)

Mi—patschen
Sol—clap
La—touch shoulders
Re—squat down on heels, arms out in front, hands up in sliding position.
Do—squat down on heels, rap floor with fists.

Groundhog Day

(February 2)   *Anonymous*

Emphasis:

- finger play
- speech
- up and down
- scale song

"If, in the second month, *(Hold up 2 fingers of right hand.)*

And, on the second day, *(Hold up 2 fingers of left hand.)*

Mr. Groundhog sees his shadow, *(Make hole with index finger and thumb of R.H., slip index finger of L.H. through it.)*

Sweet springtime will delay. *(Palms out, shake head sadly.)*

But if the clouds are dark *(Pass L. hand over R. fist.)* and cover up the sun,

Then winter will be over *(Make spreading motion, both hands, palms down)*

And we can have more fun!!" *(Clap hands.)*

Scale Song (for numbered bells*)

8—lay.	8—But if the clouds are
7—springtime will de-	7—dark, and
6—shadow sweet	6—cover up the
5—Groundhog sees his	5—sun, then
4—day, Mr.	4—winter will be
3—on the second	3—over, and
2—month, and	2—we can have more
1—If in the second	1—fun.

*Strike indicated bell on underlined words

George Washington

Source unknown

Tones Used:

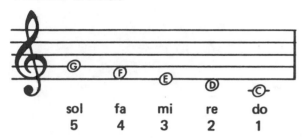

sol	fa	mi	re	do
5	4	3	2	1

February Rhythm—M.L.

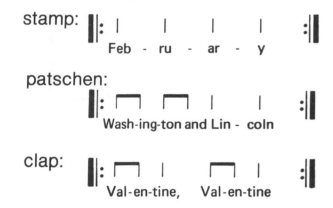

stamp:

Feb - ru - ar - y

patschen:

Wash-ing-ton and Lin - coln

clap:

Val - en-tine, Val - en-tine

make heart with hands:

Love!

Emphasis:

- older children may use as canon, with words and body percussion, or body percussion only

- may use rhythm instruments for each part

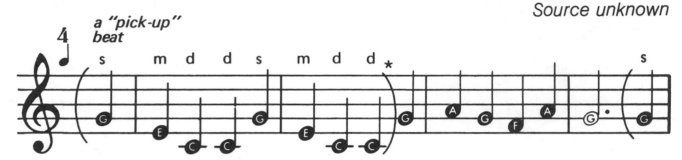

a "pick-up" beat

s   m   d   d   s   m   d   d   *   s

George Wash-ing-ton, George Wash-ing-ton, we hon-or you to - day, George

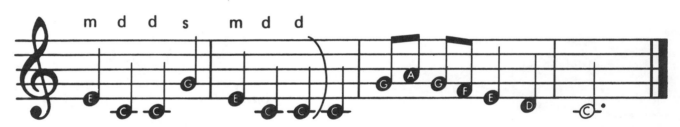

m   d   d   s   m   d   d

Wash-ing-ton, George Wash-ing-ton, the Fa-ther of the U. S. A.

*Use arm signals on these parts:

Sol (clap) *Mi* (patschen) *Do* (rap sides of chair with fists)

Do this as a motion only; do not name syllables at this stage.

♩ -Ta-a-a

Rabbit Rhythms

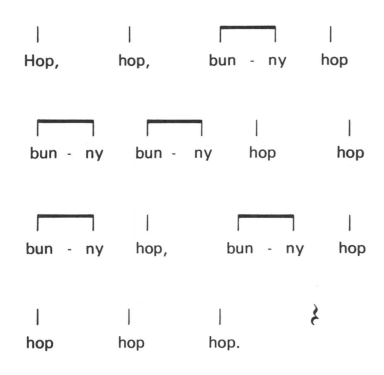

Hop, hop, bun - ny hop

bun - ny bun - ny hop hop

bun - ny hop, bun - ny hop

hop hop hop.

- T. chant, children echo
- T. chant and clap rhythm, children echo
- T. clap rhythm only, children echo

Extension:

- T. claps a rhythm. "Which words did I clap?"
- T. *chants* a rhythm, Ch. *clap* the echo.
- Alternate words for above patterns:

    "Eggs, Eggs, Easter Eggs."

Words with 3 sounds	Words with 2 sounds
cottontail	bunny
chocolate	rabbit
bunnytrail	basket
daffodil	flower
hippity	hopping

Use echo—first the 3's then the 2's

- T. chant, children echo
- T. chant and clap, children echo

Extension: combine 3's and 2's.

- use *accent* on a 3 syllable word:

    $\overset{>}{\text{Daf}}$-fo-dil - $\overset{>}{\text{Daf}}$-fo-dil - $\overset{>}{\text{Daf}}$-fo-dil

- "Superbrains" can chant and clap accented syllables only

Eight Little Bunnies

Drawing on the beat

Hip - pi - ty hop and | hip - pi - ty hay, | eight lit - tle bun - nies | out to play,

Hip - pi - ty hop and | hip - pi - ty hay, | one lit - tle bun - ny | runs a - way.

Continue: seven, six, etc.

On last verse: Hippety, Hop, and Hippety *Ho,* Where did all the bunnies go?
                    Hippety, Hop, and Hippety *Ho,* Only the Easter Bunny knows.

Make drawing strokes on the
steady beats 1 and 4 on all eight rabbits for 8 verses:

1)

2)

3) (heads)

4) left ears

5) (right ears)

6) tails

7) (whiskers)

8)

9) erase one
by one

Additional Resource Materials

1. Andress, Barbara, *Music Experiences in Early Childhood*
   Holt, Rinehart & Winston, 1980

2. Bacon, Denise, *Let's Sing Together* $2.00
   Songs for three, four, and five year olds.
   Boosey & Hawkes, Oceanside, NJ 11572

3. Burnett, Millie, *Melody, Movement, and Language* $5.95
   Music in game form for pre-school and primary grades.
   Belwin Mills

4. Choksy, Lois, *The Kodaly Method*
   Prentice-Hall, Inc., Englewood Cliffs, NJ.

5. Darazs, Arpad, *Sight and Sound*
   Teacher's Ed., and Student's Manual
   Boosey and Hawkes

6. Erdei, Peter, *150 American Folk Songs to Sing and Play*, $7.50
   Boosey and Hawkes

7. Gillespie, Avon, *Zing, Zing, Zing*   75¢
   Album: In Workshop With Avon Gillespie, $6.95
   Bellwin Mills

8. Jones, Bessie & Hawes, *Step It Down* $10.00
   Harper & Rowe (excellent source book)

9. Kenney, Maureen, *Circle Round the Zero*
   Play chants and singing games.
   Magnamusic—Baton, Inc., St. Louis, MO 53132

10. Kidd, Eleanor, *Threshold to Music*, Second Ed.
    Large charts and Teachers' Guides, three levels
    Fearon Publishers, 6 Davis Dr.,
    Belmont, CA 94002

11. Lewis, Aden G., *Listen, Look, and Stop*, Vols. 1, 2, and 3
    Teacher's Ed., Large charts accompany.
    Silver-Burdett

12. Nash, Grace, *Creative Approach to Child Development With Music, Language, and Movement*
    Today With Music, K-3, large charts available.
    Alfred Publishing Co., 15335 Morrison St., P.O. Box 5964, Sherman Oaks, CA 91413

13. Nash, Jones, Potter, Smith, *Do It My Way—The Child's Way of Learning*,   Alfred Publishing Co., Inc.

14. Orff-Schulwerk, American Education, *Music for Children*, Vol. 2, Primary;   Schott Music Corp.

15. Richards, Mary Helen, *The Child in Depth*
    (This is recommended for Kindergarten teachers, also good for administration reinforcement. Contains a superintendent's statement.) 149 Carte Madera Road., Pertola Valley, CA 94025

16. Richards, Mary Helen, *Threshold to Music*
    Contains large charts beginning with Kindergarten and going through third. One "starting" chart for middle grades. Teacher's Manual. Pentatonic song book, teacher training record and other supplementary aids.
    6 Davis Drive, Belmont, CA 94002, 1964

17. Lewis, Aden, *Basic Skills in Music,* Words, Letters, Numbers, Miscellaneous, record, book, game cards. Alfred Publishing Co., Inc.

18. Pratt, Rosalie and Peterson, Meg, *Elementary Music for All Learners,* Teacher's book, Student book, charts, records, Alfred Publishing Co., Inc.

Index

*Songs